Green-Collar Jobs

Other Northwest Environment Watch Titles

Tax Shift

Over Our Heads: A Local Look at Global Climate

Misplaced Blame: The Real Roots of Population Growth

Stuff: The Secret Lives of Everyday Things

The Car and the City

This Place on Earth: Home and the Practice of Permanence

Hazardous Handouts: Taxpayer Subsidies to Environmental Degradation

State of the Northwest

GREEN-COLLAR JOBS

Working in the New Northwest

Alan Thein Durning

RESEARCH ASSISTANCE BY
Nicholas Dankers
Judith Kmileck
Meg O'Leary
Owen Reynolds
Leila Sievanen

NEW REPORT 8
NORTHWEST ENVIRONMENT WATCH ◆ SEATTLE

Northwest Environment Watch is an independent, not-for-profit research center in Seattle, Washington, with an affiliated charitable organization, NEW BC, in Victoria, British Columbia. Their joint mission: to foster a sustainable economy and way of life throughout the Pacific Northwest—the biological region stretching from southern Alaska to northern California and from the Pacific Ocean to the crest of the Rockies. Northwest Environment Watch is founded on the belief that if northwesterners cannot create an environmentally sound economy in their home place—the greenest corner of history's richest civilization—then it probably cannot be done. If they can, they will set an example for the world.

Library of Congress Catalog Card Number: 99-61630
ISBN 1-886093-08-3

Cover design and interior illustration: Cathy Schwartz
Cover photo: Redwoods along California's Redwood Highway, © 1999 Steve Sullivan.
Map: Cynthia Thomas, based on Conservation International and Ecotrust, "Original Distribution of Coastal Temperate Rain Forests of North America," Portland, 1991
Interior photo: Ketchikan's mill, courtesy Alan Thein Durning
Editing and composition: Ellen W. Chu
Proofreading: Sherri Schultz

Printed by Alpha One Corporation, Redmond, Washington, with vegetable-based ink on recycled paper. Text: 100 percent postconsumer waste, bleached with hydrogen peroxide. Cover: 50 percent preconsumer waste, bleached with hydrogen peroxide.

Northwest Environment Watch is a 501(c)(3) tax-exempt organization. To order Northwest Environment Watch titles or to become a member, please contact us:

Northwest Environment Watch, 1402 Third Avenue, Suite 1127, Seattle, WA 98101-2118 USA; (206) 447-1880; fax (206) 447-2270; e-mail *new@northwestwatch.org;* Web *www.northwestwatch.org*

NEW BC, P.O. Box 42076, 2200 Oak Bay Avenue, Victoria, BC V8R 6T4 Canada; (250) 595-0577; fax (250) 595-0575; e-mail *newbc@home.com*

CONTENTS

KETCHIKAN

Closing the Mill

TO THE TEENAGERS FILING INTO KETCHIKAN HIGH School this dark morning through a tentative pause in the southeast Alaskan rains, the future looks different than it did to their counterparts a decade ago. In the late eighties, Ketchikan was the staging ground for a logging bonanza, and timber employment in Alaska was setting new records. If you had a good work ethic and a strong back, you could drop out of high school and make more money than your teacher.

But today—a cold November Monday in 1998—the southeast Alaskan timber industry has shrunk to one-third its peak employment, and almost nobody at "K High" is staking much on wood fiber. Nissa Cleman, whose father runs a logging company, has no intention of following him into the business. Rusty Etten, whose father was laid off from the town's pulp mill, does not see timber in his future. And Lindsey

Barnes says, "I was thinking about studying environmental sciences, which is pretty weird since I'm from this pulp mill town."[1]

All three, like most students here, are bound for college. All accept the fact that the global, information economy now demands at least 16 years of formal education. Their principal, Anthony Kennedy, practically chants "high skill, high pay" at them. In the sixties, he worked his way through college in the mills of Coeur d'Alene, Idaho. He says, "I did seven different jobs in the mill. Six out of seven no longer exist; they've been automated."

Ketchikan's easy-street timber jobs are also gone. The final blow came in March 1997, when the Ketchikan Pulp Company shut its mill and laid off almost 500 workers. Most of them, the elite of Alaska's manufacturing laborers, were well paid but poorly educated. They received an average of $45,000 a year for doing their part in the conversion of old-growth forests to dissolving pulp—a chemical building block of rayon, cellophane, and certain explosives.[2]

Northwest media described the showdown preceding the mill closure as a classic case of jobs versus the environment, the latest skirmish of the war in the woods made famous by the spotted owl. Or they described it as another instance of a broader, purportedly incessant struggle between economy and environment.

I am visiting Northwest timber towns this fall and winter trying to better understand this supposed conflict. The journey is helping me personalize the mammoth body of economic literature and research data published on the subject. And it is helping me think about one of the Pacific Northwest's most confounding challenges: if we are going to safeguard most remaining natural ecosystems, stop sprawl, slash greenhouse gas emissions, curtail toxic chemicals, clean the air and water, and save endangered species, just what is everyone going to do for a living? In particular, what can the Northwest do to help its hard-pressed rural areas sustain their economies without high-volume resource extraction?

My answers to these questions are only partial, but they are guardedly optimistic. Employment and conservation are more often complementary than antagonistic, and most apparent conflicts between them disappear under rigorous examination. With surprising speed, Northwest employment is uncoupling itself from the volume businesses of resource extraction. The blistering pace of technological change, particularly the information revolution, has meant that most new jobs are in industries that spin wealth not by moving more timber or steel—at least not within the Northwest—but by moving electrons, or stimulating neurons, in more profitable ways. Steadily, the economy is becoming more about qualities than quantities, and the ascendant industries, while not without environmental problems, pollute less, consume fewer resources, and disrupt less habitat per job and per dollar of sales than do the declining industries. So although the transition from hewing wood to crafting bytes does not cure the Northwest's ecological ills, it makes their cure easier: the typical Northwest job is gentler to ecosystems than it used to be.

Unfortunately, the good news is tempered with two kinds of bad: the new Northwest has wider income disparities than the old Northwest had, and the consumption patterns of the winners in the new economy are quickly displacing the production patterns of the old industries as environmental threats. The things we are paid to do pose a smaller problem; the things we pay to do pose a bigger one. Thus, greening our work may prove simpler than greening our lifestyles—or than sustaining a modicum of income equality.

The best-case scenario is a future that blends advanced technology with humane policies to meet the region's millennial challenge: making the Northwest a global model of prosperity, prosperity that is shared among all citizens and abides by nature's limits.

The worst-case scenario, equally possible, is a bipolar economy: high-paying, long-hour, relatively green information-age work for those hooked into the global market and low-paying, temporary jobs for those who are not. This future, already manifest in places, includes trophy homes; telecommuting; second-home sprawl; and jet-setting, recreational consumerism for the privileged. For the not-so-privileged, it offers daily job insecurity, falling wages, and trailer parks. Furthermore, this emerging dystopia exports many of its environmental impacts beyond the boundaries of the Pacific Northwest, through the global production lines for goods such as Range Rovers and petroleum.

The Northwest's boundaries, defining the focus of this book, stretch from southeast Alaska to northern California—along a coastline cloaked in the largest rain forests outside the tropics—and inland to the headwaters of the rain-forest rivers (map inside front cover). This area, a biological zone of waterways home to salmon, is a test case for green livelihoods. Once overwhelmingly dependent on logging and other forms of resource extraction, the Northwest—with 14 million inhabitants, 7 million workers, and a $350 billion gross regional product—is now at the leading edge of both the conservation movement and the global information economy.[3]

I am visiting Northwest places that are in different stages of the transition from timber to information to learn about the promise and pitfalls of this metamorphosis. I have chosen timber not because the industry is especially important to the Northwest economy, but because it is important to how the Northwest thinks about its economy. To many northwesterners, logging—and not farming, fishing, manufacturing, or any of the other possible case studies—epitomizes the supposed conflict between jobs and environment.

For me, for this book, the timber industry is a lens for viewing the larger economy. My hunch is that the uneasy transition the region's timber towns have been making holds lessons about how all northwesterners can reconcile work and nature. This book documents the efforts of remarkable northwesterners who are leading this change—by planning community forestry, fostering value-added manufacturing, retraining workers for ecosystem restoration, tapping the conservation market, and tethering money at home. None of these approaches is sufficient in itself, but they underline an all-important lesson: people make the economy, and people can change it.

THE JOBS-VERSUS-ENVIRONMENT drama has played out dozens of times in recent decades in the Northwest, usually according to the same script: representatives of declining resource industries predict economic catastrophe unless business continues as usual; there's a flurry of publicity; politicians make bold proclamations; and then, when people have stopped paying attention, expansion in the Northwest economy quickly offsets lost resource jobs. Unfortunately, the new jobs bring problems of their own.

This morning I have been wondering whether Ketchikan is any different. After all, it is on an island where rain is measured by the foot, two hours by plane from any major city. Alternatives to pulp seem few. What I am learning is that Ketchikan, far from being exceptional, is a microcosm for the entire Northwest.

The Ketchikan Pulp Company's mill is a billion-dollar complex of outsized machinery on a sheltered inlet five miles north of town. Nestled between dark slopes and darker waters, the facility is silent today—a fitting symbol for the Northwest's extractive industries. Before the pulp company turned this site over to experts in industrial decontamination, the mill chewed and boiled through the logs from hundreds of square miles of old-growth woodlands in the Tongass National Forest. The Tongass, which stretches over the thousand-island archipelago of the Alaskan panhandle, holds close to one-third of North America's unlogged temperate rain forest. The Tongass is to the Pacific Northwest as the Northwest is to North America: sparsely populated, wet, and relatively unspoiled.[4]

In the fifties, the U.S. Forest Service offered a half-century contract for cheap logs to anyone who would make pulp here. Ketchikan Pulp signed up for these unprecedented terms, gaining the largest exclusive logging rights on any U.S. government land. Federal subsidies fueled the cut in the eighties, and production rose to a peak in 1990. Then Congress trimmed the subsidies, and the Forest Service tightened environmental controls on logging. In Alaska, a tectonic shift was under way in resource stewardship. The change was piecemeal and compromised, but ecosystem management, not extraction, became the official mission of public-lands agencies.

Again, with variations in details, the same story could be told for the Northwest overall.[5]

By 1995, Ketchikan's mill was in trouble. The market for dissolving pulp was weak; log supplies were tight; and after some of its workers blew the whistle on the company's illegal waste discharges, the company pleaded guilty to violating air and water standards. The facility, never terribly profitable, needed about $200 million in improvements to stay open. In 1996, its Portland-based owners, Louisiana Pacific, issued an ultimatum to the Forest Service: tack 15 years onto the company's 50-year contract, or Ketchikan would be out its largest employer.[6]

Par for the course, everyone from Ketchikan business owners to Alaskan leaders sided with Louisiana Pacific. Ketchikan's local government even appropriated $1 million to lobby Congress. Business leaders prophesied doom. Mark Suwyn, chief executive at Louisiana Pacific, predicted, "The area will be economically devastated within three to five years." The Alaska Department of Labor forecast that the unemployment rate could "easily double" to more than 15 percent after the mill closed. Politicians made bold proclamations. Alaska's U.S. Senator Frank Murkowski declared, "I cannot stand idly by and watch the town of Ketchikan die." But nothing would convince Washington, D.C., to blink under Louisiana Pacific's stare. If the mill could not both obey the law and survive in the market, there was nothing the federal government could do—besides supply some transitional aid to the community.[7]

And, as elsewhere, doom has failed to show up. All over town, people are surprisingly ambivalent about the loss of the mill. Some people miss friends who moved away, but many comment on a surge of new construction in town. At the convenience store across from the mill, Mallory, the middle-aged woman behind the counter, says sales are down substantially and her hours have been cut, but a steady stream of pickups still pulls into the lot.

Nearby, at the Ketchikan Careers Transition Center, which seeks to smooth the change for mill workers, lifelong resident and former mill staffer Maxine Doyle insists the town has not yet felt the full effects. Severance pay, early retirement benefits, unemployment insurance, and state and federal aid packages have, she says, kept the economy buzzing. Jerry Collins, who worked 35 years at the mill, has seen some good in the shutdown: "Younger folks got training that allowed them to get better jobs." But many workers have had a hard time making house payments.

"We had anticipated a much bigger impact than we've felt," says city of Ketchikan finance director Bob Newel, whose town-hall office is across the street from the waterfront in Ketchikan's small downtown. "We haven't seen any drop in sales tax revenues." At the local newspaper, publisher Tena Williams notes that some businesses have lost half their revenue, but the overall impact has not been as big as predicted. New private investments and state road projects have taken up the slack.

The data confirm public perceptions. The unemployment rate rose from 8.7 percent in 1996 to 9.1 percent in 1997—the year the mill closed—then fell to 7.1 percent in 1998. Population has dipped as about one-third of the laid-off workers left town. Fast-rising real estate prices have stabilized or edged downward a few percent. But much of the blame for the slow times falls to depressed Asian markets for

Alaskan fish. Seafood-processing jobs have declined more than timber jobs in the past two years. Meanwhile, construction, grocery sales, and new-car sales have grown at double-digit paces since the mill closed. And tourism has continued to increase at an astonishing rate: more than half a million cruise ship passengers visited town in the summer of 1998—25 percent more than in 1996. Most of these shifts, especially the widening role of cars and tourism, reflect important regional trends.[8]

Ketchikan has also had growth in niche wood-product manufacturing—another regional trend. When the pulp company held most of the timber, it was hard for competitors to get raw materials. Now two independent sawmills are installing facilities. Small, flexible, and specialized, these mills will cater to markets that big operators cannot fill. Already, a few miles south of Ketchikan, in Saxman Seaport, a long-haired diesel mechanic named Gregory, who used to fix logging machinery, is turning red cedar scraps into salad bowls. Alaska Forest Creations, which caters to gourmet stores in the lower 48, pays him $11 an hour, a wage he stretches by living in his camper. Unfortunately, as throughout the region, manufacturing wages have polarized just like wages in every other sector. Even an experienced, medium-skill worker like Gregory cannot find a high-paying job anymore.

Overall, closing the pulp mill, in combination with a sharp downturn in Asian markets, has taken the boom out of Ketchikan, but it hasn't done worse. When settled families are forced to move, it's a terrible loss, and such moves are all too common. But many of the people who left Ketchikan were not settled. One-fifth of pulp jobs were held by seasonal residents, along with half of logging jobs.[9]

Furthermore, the layoffs continued a decade-long trend. Employment in every part of the southeast Alaskan private sector is at or above 1990 levels, except for the timber

What's Growing? Tourism

Tourism has been surging in the Northwest. The tourism industry in Montana overtook logging and mining combined in the early nineties. And sometime in the mid-nineties in the Pacific Northwest overall, the burgeoning travel industry appears to have grown larger in economic output than timber, mining, and fishing combined. The leisure travel market is roughly two-thirds the size of the resource industries. And leisure travel combined with recreation rivals the resource sector.[10]

Tourism, like the Northwest's other growth stars, is a mixed blessing. Its ups and downs are more predictable than timber's, and at least in Alaska, tourism jobs go overwhelmingly to permanent residents, not to seasonal visitors as in the timber industry. But tourism sacrifices towns' privacy and opens their living spaces to throngs of affluent visitors, augmenting class resentments. Like other growth sectors, tourism offers low wages for low skill, and it is seasonal.[11]

Tourism does not clearcut ancient forests or strip-mine landscapes, but it does degrade the environment in other ways. Cruise ships that ply the waters off Ketchikan, while generally a resource-efficient form of travel, have repeatedly dumped waste oil at sea. And tourism, which accounts for about 10 percent of the region's driving and one-quarter of its air travel, produces an estimated 5 percent of the Northwest's emissions of climate-changing gases. (Old-growth logging produces 10 percent.)[12]

industry. Tourism has been the growth star, expanding about 5 percent each year. This year, tourism employs four times as many people as the timber industry, and it may now have surpassed seafood to become southeast Alaska's largest industry. Still, in Ketchikan it is disdained, for legitimate reasons. At the Pioneer Pantry in the town's tourism district, where shops point their quaint facades at the cruise ship dock, a waitress named Gladys says, with regret bordering on contempt, "*Tourism* is what we live off now."[13]

FROM KETCHIKAN SOUTH to California's redwood coast, the region's old economy has withered. Since the early seventies, more than 500 lumber, pulp, and paper mills have closed, cutting the total by 38 percent; the fleet of fishing boats has shrunk by 8,000—a 45 percent reduction; and more than 15,000 farms and ranches have gone out of business, a decline of 12 percent. (The number of mines, meanwhile, has nearly doubled to 1,300, but the growth has been in small quarries. Mining employment has plunged since 1981.)[14]

The Northwest's natural resource industries—counting fishing, mining, and the whole timber industry from forestry to paper milling—have shed 71,000 jobs from their absolute peak of 369,000 jobs 20 years ago, and their contribution to the income of Northwest households, adjusted for inflation, has declined by 31 percent. Meanwhile, services and other knowledge-intensive employment sectors have been surging. Overall, the region's economy has added almost 3 million jobs—a 56 percent increase—since 1979. As a result, extraction's relative importance has fallen steeply. In 1972, the resource industries accounted for 9 percent of Northwest jobs; in 1997, they accounted for less than 4 percent. In 1979, they supplied northwesterners with 11 percent of their personal income; in 1996, they supplied 5 percent.[15]

Thus, to an extent that few people realize, the Northwest is no longer a resource extraction economy. The old industries of logging, mining, and fishing have dwindled to a small share of the region's total economy, slipping downward on the league list of employment sectors. In total jobs and in total personal income, for example, they slipped below finance, insurance, and real estate in the early eighties; below health care in the late eighties; and below business services (such as accounting and computer software) in the late nineties. Some parts of the Pacific Northwest, including rural British Columbia and several remote counties of the Northwest states, are behind the rest of the region in this transition, but they are on the same path.[16]

According to the conventional view of how the economy works—a view still embedded in the models employed by some government agencies—the entire Northwest should be in the pits by now. With the alleged locomotive of the regional economy running short of steam, pink slips should be everywhere. But in almost all of the Northwest's cities, and even in many of its rural areas, the economy has thrived during the progressive dismantling of the supposed job base. As 1998 ended, unemployment rates were the lowest in a quarter century in much of the Northwest, and few parts of North America had a better jobs outlook over the long term.[17]

What has happened is the information revolution. In the Pacific Northwest, the natural resources that most matter to the economy are no longer little-processed raw exports but the natural amenities the region offers to workers in high-value industries. Companies that code software, manufacture computer components, design and assemble airplanes, write legal briefs, shoot movies, process foods, publish information, sell things on the Internet, clean up industrial waste sites, and finance and insure all of the above—these businesses are

The Work Place

The contours of work in the Northwest have shifted markedly in the past 25 years. The share of adults who work for pay has rarely been larger: some 79 percent of adult northwesterners hold paid jobs. Most of the remainder, of course, are also working; they're just not getting paid. Perhaps a quarter of all economic activity occurs in the household and voluntary economies, not the money economy.[18]

Of the Northwest's 6.8 million workers, only 3 million toil full time in the world of large corporate businesses. More than 2 million draw their paychecks from small businesses, those with fewer than 50 employees. Nearly 1 million are self-employed, and another million are in the public sector.[19]

Work arrangements are increasingly varied. The full-time, lifelong job is a thing of the past. Since the late eighties, the number of people in the United States whose work is less than full time has quadrupled. In the Northwest, 21 percent of workers are part-timers. Temporary workers are among the fastest-growing groups, their numbers jumping four times faster than jobs overall in Washington between 1982 and 1995. In Oregon between 1980 and 1994, the temporary-help industry expanded seven times faster than the economy overall. In British Columbia, one-fifth of workers are self-employed, up from one-eighth two decades ago. And people change jobs more often: typical American workers now switch jobs a dozen times during their working lives.[20]

the vanguard of the Northwest economy. They deal more in ideas, expertise, and information than in bulky commodities. Their most valuable properties are not landholdings, mineral deposits, or billion-dollar factories but patents, copyrights, and brands.

In this economy of mind, not matter, businesses must compete for talented workers as well as markets, and attractive locations give would-be employers a leg up. In a way, then, quality of life is the new commodity boom in the Northwest. Healthy, attractive ecosystems are, in addition to their biological value to human survival, as important a part of the economic infrastructure as silicon chips or ocean ports. All of the region's growth sectors—recreation, tourism, retirement, real estate, high tech, health care, business services—depend on the place to provide great views, friendly communities, pleasant weather, rich cultural offerings, inviting trails, safe streets, and efficient infrastructure. They need quality of life as much as loggers need trees.[21]

In environmental impacts, the Northwest's industries divide into three tiers. Measured per dollar of sales, businesses at the economy's feeding end—those that extract and process natural resources—are the Northwest's highest-impact firms. Because they specialize in matter, the Northwest's dams, farms, logging companies, pulp and paper mills, mines, power plants, aluminum smelters, and metal and petroleum refineries take a toll on the region's environment out of proportion to their numbers. Among them are the league leaders in energy and water consumption, habitat disruption, toxic waste generation, and air and water pollution. Yet they employ few workers per dollar of output, accounting in total for one Northwest job in ten, and the number has been shrinking.[22]

The medium-impact, second-tier industries—construction and land development, manufacturing, trucking and air travel—also share disproportionately in transgressions against nature. These slow-growing industries employ slightly more workers per dollar of output than the high-impact industries and account for just over two jobs in ten in the Northwest.[23]

The labor-intensive service sectors, such as education, finance, government, and health care, form the low-impact tier of employers. These fast-growing industries account for seven in ten Northwest jobs. Jobs in business services have tripled since 1979, as have jobs in the amusement and recreation industry. Education, health care, and personal services have all doubled their job counts.[24]

This ranking of industries is intended to illuminate how job trends affect the environment, not to assign blame. Yet it obscures some facts: certain companies in every sector are better or worse than the norm. For example, organic farmers, selective loggers, and paper recyclers are not high-impact enterprises, while nuclear medicine departments, lawn care providers, and dry cleaners—all service industries—are not low impact. Moreover, industries in the three tiers are linked. Educators use paper; software improvements drive a throwaway economy in computer hardware; and bankers finance everything else.

Finally, and most important, consumers, not producers, cause a rising share of environmental harm: urban air pollution, for example, comes mostly from tailpipes, and most driving (and most growth in driving) now consists of people taking to the roads for reasons unrelated to work. Similarly, the region's armies of woodstoves, power mowers, and barbecue grills constitute growing threats to air quality, just as leaks from septic tanks and crankcases make up an increasing share of water pollution.[25]

Still, the recent Northwest job shifts—decline among high-impact industries, slow growth among medium-impact industries, and rapid growth among low-impact industries—

What's Happening? Globalization

Commerce has become global in recent decades, with foreign trade growing several times faster than the North American economy overall. International sales of stocks and bonds have grown even faster. Americans alone bought and sold foreign stocks and bonds worth more than twice the U.S. gross national product in 1997; in 1975, such sales equaled only 2 percent of GNP.[26]

The Pacific Northwest is especially active in trade: the region that some call Ecotopia might be more aptly named Exportopia. Washington is among the most trade-dependent states in the nation. British Columbia's sales have shifted dramatically toward the Pacific Rim. One-third of British Columbia's exports go to Asia, and almost all of those are natural resources pouring out of the region's busiest port, Vancouver.[27]

Globalization has its domestic counterpart in the nationalization of regional economies. Purchases and sales that cross the borders of Washington State, for example, have increased more quickly than the state economy since the sixties. More than one-third of dollars spent by Washington consumers go straight out of the state. A similar share of greater Portland's purchasing dollars leaves the metropolitan area, and all but 3 percent of these escaping dollars leap over the city's rural periphery into national and international markets. (Studies are environmental boons. If these changes had not occurred, the region's landscape would be in much worse shape. The big question is whether other, faraway landscapes are paying the price. Perhaps the Northwest's economic transition simply transfers environmental impacts abroad. Perhaps

on Portland, Seattle, and Idaho Falls, Idaho, have found astonishingly little economic interaction between metropolitan areas and their rural hinterlands.) Thus, money is decreasingly local; it flits around with extraordinary agility. And many businesses in both urban and rural parts of the Northwest sell as much into national and international markets as into regional ones.[28]

The rise of so-called big-box stores such as Wal-Mart or Home Depot—the biggest retailing trend of the nineties in the Pacific Northwest—is another prime example of the decline of local economies. Big-box chains slash costs by centralizing inventory and purchasing at large distribution facilities, bypassing local economies. Big-box retailers now account for three-quarters of all sales by general merchandisers in British Columbia. In agriculture, similar trends are evident. The 2 percent of farms that grow 40 percent of American crops have mostly severed their links to local suppliers of seeds, fertilizers, and services such as financing and marketing. Instead, they operate in an international marketplace, dealing directly with other giant firms. Health care, banking, and many other sectors of the Northwest economy, especially the rural economy, have gone through the same metamorphosis in recent times, consolidating, centralizing, and automating. The advent of electronic commerce is hastening this trend.[29]

northwesterners are becoming supervisors rather than tradespeople in the global division of labor, without reducing the size of the shadow they cast on the global environment.

The available evidence suggests that most of the economic change in the Northwest has followed from a shifting mix of consumption in North America, not from moving high-impact activities offshore. While not trimming their use per person of natural resources, northwesterners are not adding to it very much. Efficiency improvements and upscaling tastes have balanced one another in buildings and vehicles, for example, leaving per capita resource use flat. Per capita energy consumption in the region has been hovering around the same level since the early seventies. (Unfortunately, total resource consumption remains unsustainably high, and reducing it is North America's principal environmental challenge.) So, while economic globalization has certainly left the Northwest exporting a somewhat larger share of its environmental impacts, its jobs shift must still be counted a plus for the global environment. Were such a shift not taking place, the planet's condition would be even more precarious.[30]

IN A BARN-RED building next to the town's diminutive shopping mall, employees of the Ketchikan Jobs Center vastly outnumber job seekers. A bewildered 41-year-old logger pokes at a late-model computer terminal on the fourth floor, attempting to discover any job postings for which he might qualify. What's a high-tech economy got to offer the working class? "There's jobs," he says, "but they're all skilled. There's no jobs for a guy like me." His name is Blu Davis.

"I've been a logger for 24 years," he says. Blu finished eighth grade near Astoria, Oregon, where his mother now runs a beauty college, then dropped out to work on a neighbor's dairy farm. At 17, he went to his first logging camp and liked the lifestyle. "You could live how you wanted. If you didn't like one guy's camp, you could go to another one." He worked in a Ketchikan Pulp Company camp, among other places. In the 11 years he's lived in Ketchikan, he has also fished part of the year, but new fishing rules now deny him a permit.

"It used to be there was always something to do. I could just call up the Jobs Center, and they'd tell me where to go. It was nothing to make $100 a day on a boat or $150 a day in a camp. But you can't get a job like that anymore." Automation and decline in the timber and fishing industries have left Blu on unemployment insurance and doing carpentry jobs when he can get them.

I ask him if he's gone through any of the retraining programs offered here at the Jobs Center. He sneers at the thought. "Here they teach you how to run a cash register and a credit card machine to work in somebody's curio shop for $6 an hour and still get laid off in October." Blu is particularly mystified by high tech, saying he doesn't "believe in the electronic society. You can't talk to a human being anymore. It's all computers now."

Since the Jobs Center began posting jobs online instead of on the wall, Blu has been bringing his 12-year-old son with him to help operate the computer. Today, he is trying on his own, and he pushes buttons for several minutes. Soon he gives up and leaves. His terminal shows that he could not figure out how to log on to the database.

To people like Blu, the economy is something that happens to you, like the weather or an epidemic. And today the information economy is happening to him. Somewhere offshore in the waters where he once fished, a ship called the *Global Sentinel,* bristling with satellite and sonar navigation gear, is inching its way from Juneau down a sheltered water route called the Inside Passage. It's heading for Seattle, playing out southeast Alaska's first fiber-optic cable on the seabed behind it. The cord, which is no thicker than Blu's thumb, will eventually carry 130,000 telephone and modem calls at a time, giving southeast Alaska its own on-ramp to the information superhighway.

The unheralded passage of this ship is probably the most important thing to happen to southeast Alaska's economy this month. The strand submerging under the waves is connecting this humid slice of cold jungle to the new economy. It's also connecting rural Alaska to a metropolis, which is what helps rural areas prosper.[31]

Urban districts hold 68 percent of the Northwest's population, and a larger share of its jobs. The global economy may not recognize national boundaries, but it certainly recognizes great cosmopolitan centers. Indeed, many economic development specialists now believe the economy grows principally in cities, because of the explosive synergies of innovation they unleash. New wealth, in other words, is nowadays mostly a product not of rural zones but of urban ones, of their laboratories, corporate cubicles, universities, engineering firms, factories, office towers, and other work sites.[32]

Recent economic trends in the Northwest point so directly to the megalopolis stretching from Portland, Oregon, through Seattle, Washington, to Vancouver, B.C.—call it "Portcouver"—that focusing this book on outposts such as Ketchikan may seem misguided. I have done so because the task of reconciling work and nature is most daunting in resource towns. They have virtually everything against them. In a global economy, competition squeezes the old rural economy of commodities the hardest. Compared with their urban competitors, rural businesses face higher costs and longer delays. They rely on a workforce that is, on average, less educated than the urban one. Almost all the trends favor metropolitan areas: they are the natural home to health care, high tech, business services, and other growth sectors. Greater Vancouver's share of all jobs in British Columbia, for example, just keeps rising; the city has outperformed the rest of the province through good times and bad.[33]

Rural areas' strengths in the decades ahead will be in providing amenities that more-developed areas cannot, such as solitude, wildness, and beauty. Across the Northwest, the fastest-growing rural districts are those on the edges of metropolitan zones and those favored for recreation and retirement. Rural counties with heavy concentrations of resource extraction and farming are the ones suffering.[34]

KETCHIKAN CLINGS TO the serpentine walls of a mountainous island, as if a naval armada had broken apart offshore and washed up on the tide. For several miles north and south, buildings perch not far above salt water. One afternoon I follow a school bus, empty but for three passengers, up a bobsled track of a road posted "chains required" and find the town dump. Possibly the world's most scenic landfill, it sits on a bench above town with million-dollar views of peaks and surf. And beside it is Deer Mountain Trailer Park, home to many of Ketchikan's working poor. In the far rear, behind the newer double-wides, crouch a dumpster and five near-dead camper trailers on the igneous shards of a blown-out rock quarry. A hungry dog trails me. The school bus turns around. I wonder where Blu Davis lives.

A SUSTAINABLE ECONOMY can generate employment just as well as an unsustainable one. For every declining industry, like those that log old-growth forests, make farm chemicals, and build roads, there is an emerging one to take up the slack, like those that advise organic farmers, build windmills, and design walkable neighborhoods. A sustainable economy could be full of opportunity, and not only in these overtly green sectors. Mostly, a sustainable Northwest would push to its logical end the current trend toward producing and consuming services. It would be a regional workplace full of designers, analysts, creators, artists, instructors, scientists, health workers, engineers, therapists, entertainers, waiters, programmers, guides, consultants, writers, marketers, and more.

But the incremental change from the status quo to an economy that aims for ecological durability, like any major social transition, will be full of painful transformations. The new jobs often require different—and more sophisticated—skills than the old ones, and they're sometimes in different places. Sacrificing environmental quality to freeze existing jobs in place is unlikely to work. Closing Ketchikan's mill has allowed southeast Alaska's wilderness-tourism economy to thrive, created an opening for a diversified wood products industry, and secured Ketchikan's place as a world-class home address for footloose firms operating in a global market. And the mill was unlikely to survive much longer even if Congress had extended its subsidized contract. The cards were stacked against it.

Still, change hurts. The Canadian Labour Congress, recognizing what lies ahead, is developing the concept of "just transitions." Workers in high-impact industries, like most northwesterners, are proficient in their occupations, dedicated to their communities, and proud of their accomplishments. Few of them get rich from what they do, and some earn little. They deserve the support of their compatriots, the Labour Congress argues, as they make the change to sustainable livelihoods: first, through reliable unemployment insurance and retraining opportunities, and second, through community planning efforts in which they can participate.[35]

Turning our nature-blind economy into one that is, while still market-driven, at last compatible with the health of the Earth will be too wrenching a change if attention is not paid to who wins and who loses. Spurious arguments in favor of resource jobs are no more a reason to continue despoiling nature than jobs in weapons plants are a reason for war. But environmental measures that do not recognize a worker's right to a fair chance in the new economy are equally menacing to our future. A green-collar Northwest that simply shuts out Blu Davis is a high-skill enclave, not an economic model for the world.

HAIDA GWAII

Uniting the Community

On maps, the Queen Charlotte Islands look like a green powder horn pointing southeast toward the provincial capital of Victoria. From the window of this airplane, though, they look like mossy stones under the North Pacific's carpet of clouds. The remote archipelago—Haida Gwaii to the Haida people who have lived here for millennia—rarely shows itself in November, so I count myself lucky when wind sweeps the clouds aside. As the plane descends, I see snow-peppered ranges arching their backs out of the sea and sunlight glinting across the beleaguered village of Sandspit below.

The wood products industry in the Pacific Northwest is currently stuck in the worst recession since the early eighties. "The whole industry is in the tank," according to Bill Beldessi, whom I'm going to visit. Log prices are down 20 percent from a year ago. Demand for timber—as for apples, fish, wheat, and most other Northwest commodities—is slack this fall because of Asia's recession, and world prices are low. The coast and islands of British Columbia are a remaining stronghold of the Pacific Northwest's shrunken timber industry, and 43 percent of timber workers in this heartland are laid off.[36]

Commodity industries always boom and bust, but in Northwest timber, recent busts have usually brought permanent cuts in employment. When the market improves, the implacable logic of capital—which roams the globe searching for the highest rates of return—always seems to dictate automation, not rehiring. For this reason, many in the region's resource industries see this season's recession as another turn of the screw, not a passing dry spell.[37]

The only hope for reversing this tightening spiral is if the Pacific Northwest can wring more jobs from each log. The Queen Charlottes are a case study in the pitfalls of industrial extraction. They are also an object lesson in the need to replace extraction with an economy of value, not volume.

BILL BELDESSI'S BLUE king-cab pickup, like most human-made artifacts here, is held together by baling wire and hope. Still, it manages to carry us, slowly, on the short tour of Sandspit—a place as hard hit by the transition from extraction to information as any.

"The town's on the verge of folding up," Bill says. Sandspit is the logging base for most of southern Haida Gwaii. TimberWest, the company that holds the license to harvest trees in the area, has pulled out, Bill says, "after they logged the bejesus out of it." Bill should know. He hauled a lot of the logs to port. A lifelong woods worker, he's now a laid-off truck driver.

Haida Gwaii has a logging camp economy. Helicopters line the airport, ready to carry timber planners from the inbound plane to the slopes they will shave next. The felled logs ride barges to mills in British Columbia's southern cities.

Leaving the airport on Sandspit's main street, Bill points to a row of empty houses. "It's pretty desperate up here now," he says. "It's been a year since anyone worked." Some of his neighbors have taken to drinking, and he says domestic violence has increased. "About half the people have left. The population's gone from 650 to 300 in 12 months," he says. But many of the diehards are struggling to diversify. "We don't want to be in the same situation again."

Bill's Chevy stutters past the town grocer, barber, and clothing outlet, all of which are foundering as the population ebbs. It passes the local school, where the student body has plummeted; the gas station, now open just four hours a day; and the vacant offices of TimberWest, the fifth company in a decade to run logging in this part of Haida Gwaii. In British Columbia, virtually all logging takes place on public lands, not as in the Northwest states, where about half of timberlands are private. British Columbia's forest policies favor big companies, so most logging in the province is done by huge, centralized corporations.

Soon the pickup passes another string of small, empty houses facing the sea. The provincial government reports that one-quarter of personal income on the Queen Charlottes comes from timber, either directly or after industry expenditures circulate locally. The government may be right about the islands, but such figures are mostly misleading. They are derived from "economic base" models, which describe local economies as having two parts: basic, export industries and secondary, local ones. Exports bring money into the economy; local businesses recycle it. As a description of how money flows, this model is fine, but as a tool to predict the future or guide planning, it has little value. One scholarly review summed up, "Economic base models should be buried, and without prospects for resurrection."[38]

The implication of the economic base models is that communities should focus on boosting exports. Unfortunately, focusing on exports in the rural Northwest usually translates, through politics, into boosting resource extraction, often at the expense of the environmental and cultural amenities that are the principal lures to talented workers in other fields.[39]

Economies do not rise and fall with the flow of natural resource commodities. They rise and fall with the flow of innovative, entrepreneurial people, and in the Northwest, population has been flowing in mightily—growing 50 percent faster than global population. It is growing in almost every part of the region. Of the 118 counties in Idaho, Oregon, and Washington and the 30 regional districts in British Columbia, some 41 lost population during the eighties. But only 4 lost population between 1990 and 1997.[40]

This trend has defied the predictions of the critics of environmental laws. Since 1990, environmental protections have tightened in timber country. Yet rural populations have grown much more quickly during the nineties than during the eighties. Urban areas grew two and a half times faster than rural areas in the eighties, but rural areas' growth rate almost caught up with cities' in the nineties. Rural Washington has actually grown more quickly than urban Washington during that time. Without a doubt, the Northwest's rapid population increase is among its biggest environmental challenges.[41]

The great tide of humanity washing into the Pacific Northwest is not only arriving to fill jobs the region has already generated, but it is also generating jobs by arriving. Employers follow good workers as often as workers follow good jobs. And employers—many of them small companies—look for good places to live too. That's why, during the eighties, the populations of Northwest counties containing national parks and other federally protected wildlands grew almost twice as fast as counties without such protected lands.[42]

BILL BELDESSI DROPPED out of high school to join his father in the woods, and he eventually rose to the rank of faller—the logging team member who wields the saw. He logged all over the province before settling in the Charlottes. "There was so much work around," he explains, "you never put roots down. Companies operated that way, too. They came here to log off the good timber and went elsewhere while the second growth was coming back." Bill sees things changing now.

A large, ebullient man with white hair, Bill hasn't let his lack of formal education stand in the way of political action. He brought the "wise-use" movement to the province, founding Share the Rock in Sandspit. "When I came here ten years ago, it looked like somebody needed to stand up, not to fight the environmental movement but to speak for the community." Share groups emerged in other resource towns too, voicing timber workers' opposition to forest protection measures.

In 1991, Bill helped found the provincial umbrella group Share BC and served as its president for two years; local chapters proliferated during that time. But in 1993, Share BC overtly allied itself with the big timber companies by joining the industry-sponsored Forest Alliance, and Bill resigned.

Speaking for communities, Bill believed, was different from speaking for companies. "After that, I decided to get really involved on the islands." Share BC and Share the Rock are now defunct, but Bill is an elected leader on his island.

With paid work, Bill has had less success. Like Sandspit's other timber workers, he has exhausted his year of employment insurance checks and is now drawing down his retirement savings. If he doesn't get work in the next half year, he will lose his union seniority. But Bill isn't just waiting for the return of big timber. He is taking correspondence courses in business administration and aiming to turn his experience in politics into a new source of income as a mediator. "I'm hoping this training will give me the tools to stay here."

In the meantime, Bill's wife has taken a job at one of the islands' bed-and-breakfast inns. "She's the breadwinner now," he says. The women in laid-off timber families are usually the ones who take low-paying retail and service jobs. Most Northwest counties with declining resource industries have fast-rising female employment rates.[43]

We stop at a rudimentary house that serves as the Sandspit community office. Townspeople meet here to plan their future. On the walls are maps of their projects: improved water works, a short path to a beach where gray whales come to rub against the rocks, and a three-day backpacking route modeled on Vancouver Island's famous West Coast Trail. These community efforts count; in fact, commitment to place and an entrepreneurial class of local leaders are among the most important ingredients in economic development, according to the scholarly literature.[44]

Sandspit's first hope is tourism, but tourism is the tip of the iceberg in amenity-led development. It's the permanent residents who, determined to stay put, keep the larger part of the economy thriving. Even in the destination ski resort of Whitefish, Montana, the economic contribution from tourism pales in comparison with that from residents who choose to remain in the town because of the quality of life it offers.[45]

"Some of the folks who are over 50 are staying in town by taking early retirement," says Bill. Retired households are gold for local economies: they spend more locally than younger households, they do not fill the jobs they generate, they do not take up space in local schools, and their pensions and Social Security checks are recession-proof.[46]

The retired population is increasing quickly. In British Columbia, it's the fastest-growing age bracket. Older retirees are following the traditional retirement pattern of moving to the Sun Belt (in Canada, that's Victoria) or to retirement

WHAT'S HAPPENING? FEMINIZATION

The biggest change in the paid labor force in the last quarter century has been its feminization. Middle- and upper-class women joined their lower-class counterparts on the payroll. Consequently, a substantial share of job growth in some decades—notably in British Columbia in the eighties—has consisted of transferring functions such as cooking, child care, and housekeeping from the household sector to the cash sector. Without the increase in paid work by women, middle-class household income would have plummeted in the past 20 years. Although women continue to earn less than men, the pay gap has slowly narrowed, and in British Columbia at least, women have increased their presence in influential positions. In the first half of the nineties, for example, the female share of judges rose from 18 to 30 percent.[47]

centers close to their children. But as life spans have lengthened, younger retirees have begun moving to places with sun, mountains, and water, such as Kelowna, B.C.; Coeur d'Alene, Idaho; Polson, Montana; and Wenatchee, Washington. With any luck, Sandspit could ride this wave, at least holding its retirees, possibly drawing home some who have left. It's no sunbather's paradise, but for boating and fishing, you can't do much better. The retirement tide is likely to ebb somewhat during the next decade, only to flood again when the first baby boomers turn 65 in 2010. Then the Northwest will probably see a retirement boom as never before.[48]

The maps on the walls of the Sandspit community office display projects that could help the community attract visitors and retain retirees. They cannot display the larger project afoot on the islands. Bill describes an unprecedented alliance among timber workers, environmentalists, and the Haida Nation. The alliance aims to control the islands' forests locally and to catapult the islands' economy from woodlot to high-value manufacturer. To learn about that project, I talk to some of Bill's friends on the next island north.

ON A STEEP RISE above a mossy little town called Queen Charlotte City, Leslie Johnson and John Broadhead sit in a workshop behind their house and painstakingly map the islands. This building is the environmental movement's largest toehold on the archipelago, which makes it remarkable that Bill Beldessi counts Leslie and John as friends.

Leslie, who arrived in the archipelago from the prairie provinces 20 years ago, used to work in the woods. Living on a raft tied to a tugboat, she selectively logged along the periphery of the archipelago. John arrived on the islands 25 years ago and joined the Haida Nation's campaign to create a national park at the south end of the chain. Haida Gwaii, sometimes called the Galapagos of Canada, is home to rare species found nowhere else. The park movement succeeded in 1985, but it polarized communities, and, Leslie says, "environmentalists kept their heads down for ten years." Off the islands, however, John helped found several major organizations and is now chair of the provincial Sierra Club.[49]

The cozy workshop is finished exquisitely in wood, the peaked ceiling inlaid with tile-sized pieces of cedar. For a region that tallies timber by the million board feet, the Northwest has remarkably little love for wood; most Northwest buildings hide their lumber behind gypsum wallboard.[50]

On a large screen, John traces landforms and vegetation, pixel by pixel, integrating satellite images, planning documents, global information system databases, and aerial photographs. One of Leslie and John's early creations, commissioned by the Council of the Haida Nation, helped change islanders' perception of their home. John clicks some buttons, and this 1993 map unfurls down the screen. First Haida Gwaii appears in outline. Then it fills in with green, reflecting the extent of forest three decades ago. Finally, a jaundiced stain spreads down the chain, showing the clearcuts.

This map, since updated and improved, had a galvanizing effect. Four thousand copies spread throughout Haida Gwaii. Teachers posted them in their classrooms. Loggers studied them on coffee breaks. Most people concluded, as Jim Abbot, owner of one of the archipelago's two small sawmills, said recently, "We're sitting in a giant clearcut up here."

Around the same time, the B.C. government reported that the logging rate on the islands exceeded the sustainable rate by a factor of more than two, that 96 percent of logs were leaving the islands untouched by anything but a chainsaw, and that four in five jobs handling Haida Gwaii timber were off the islands. In late 1995, the government warned that the islands' timber supply was hitting the wall; soon thereafter, the government reduced the cut by one-third.[51]

The move was long overdue, according to Leslie. Excluding protected areas, about 90 percent of economically viable timber on the archipelago is already gone—a natural resource worth roughly Can$15 billion.

What most enrages Bill Beldessi is that the Queen Charlottes have shipped out so much wealth and got so little back. "You saw this town here," he says. "They've been logging here for 30 years, but there's nothing to show for it. The timber leaves the island. No benefits come back."

Extractive economies, despite the high wages of resource workers, are so volatile that they discourage investment and the economic diversification it brings. Timber towns typically end up with low average wages and a disproportionate number of poor families.[52]

In the wake of the harvest reduction, representatives of every elected body on the islands assembled to respond. Among these representatives were Bill Beldessi and Leslie Johnson. Three months of nearly continuous meetings later, they had created a blueprint for a new forest economy, called the Islands Community Stability Initiative (ICSI), and a governing body charged with building it.[53]

To the astonishment of everyone familiar with timber politics in British Columbia, ICSI called for a further reduction in logging. Towns across the province were demanding that Victoria give them more trees to cut, but ICSI insisted on getting down to a sustainable harvest in three years. It also prescribed allocating more wood to local loggers, who had been frozen out of the market by the province's rules. It called for wood products manufacturing on the islands, for a local log market that would introduce competition into the wood products industry, for a strong community voice in forest decisions, and for a comprehensive land-use plan developed with the Haida Nation.

Finally, ICSI called for a community forest on Haida Gwaii, leased to the islands' residents; held in trust by a local board of directors; and managed for recreation, culture, and wildlife as well as timber. Such a community forest would be a Trojan horse in the province's logging-rights system, which currently relies on licenses that specify mandatory production quotas. Instead, ICSI was calling for watershed-by-watershed ecosystem management, with no production quotas whatsoever. Local control of timberland makes a big difference to employment and income in rural towns.[54]

KIM DAVIDSON HAS been waiting 20 minutes to convene this evening's ICSI board meeting at the Skidegate Homemakers hall. A North Pacific windstorm has knocked enough branches onto the islands' roads that Kim could barely get to Skidegate, a Haida town close to Queen Charlotte City. He is from Old Masset, two hours away on the archipelago's northern edge. The Old Masset Haida recently elected Kim, who ran as a voice for conservation, to head their economic development council. His victory shows how closely connected the Haida believe jobs and the environment are: Old Masset's unemployment rate is near 70 percent.

Seven board members have managed to reach the hall through the winds, leaving the board one short of a quorum. Kim appears nervous. Tonight the board needs to start the final dash toward making the community forest a reality.

To him, ICSI fits nicely into the Haida Nation's agenda. "We want to have greater control over our ocean and forest resources," he says before the meeting, and ICSI is one means to that end. At the same time, the Haida are working through the courts. Recent legal precedents leave little doubt that the Haida will soon be the kingpins of natural resource policy on the Queen Charlottes.

Kim is relieved when Old Masset representative John Yeltatzie fights the door open against the wind and comes inside; they can proceed. But for a long while, the meeting seems to flail about over matters of small consequence. Acronyms are flying thick through the room, and matters of procedure seem to dominate the discussion. Gradually, there is halting progress. Building solidarity in diverse communities is time consuming.

The agenda item of greatest weight is the community forest application under the province's new Community Forest Act—an act written largely because of these people's work. The law creates, for the first time, a way for a B.C. forest community to control its land base directly. The application deadline is fast approaching.

Haida Gwaii gets just one-sixth as many jobs from each truckload of logs as the B.C. coast overall. If the Queen Charlottes could match the coast's jobs performance, in other words, it could stabilize timber employment with one-sixth the wood. Such success may be beyond reach. Experienced observers of rural development, while encouraging local niche manufacturing, are cautious not to overstate the prospects. Urban areas boast most of the advantages: quick access to markets and to marketing information, abundant labor, and the ability to command supplies from far and wide. In fact, more than half the Northwest's resource jobs are in cities.[55]

Still, Haida Gwaii, like much of the rural Northwest, could add a lot more value to its logs if it had access to them at all. ICSI has ambitious plans for selling logs from its community forest through an auction, giving locals a chance. To Kim Davidson, the resulting future seems clear. Cedar and spruce will become veneer, piano sounding boards, and guitars. Other local resources will also be processed on the islands. Salmon and black cod will be smoked. His community has already begun exporting herring roe on kelp, a traditional Haida food that is also a delicacy in Japan.

Kim is determined to bring this future to fruition. If that means steering a contentious group of fellow islanders through a meeting that is already stretching toward 10:00 P.M., so be it. He's certainly put up with worse. A 41-year-old father of three, Kim worked long days in the mills of Quesnel and, later, repairing logging-scarred watersheds near Old Masset. The hope of a restored and prosperous archipelago is worth the tedium of these meetings.

Board member Nika Brown throws a wrench in the wheels when she questions whether the communities they represent have fully agreed to the idea of a community forest. Bill Beldessi, growing exasperated, recounts the extensive process of public meetings and consultations and concludes, almost pleading, "We're at that stage when we need to go forward, or it's going to die." Kim calmly glances around the table. The point of no return is here.

John Yeltatzie speaks next, in soft tones. "I support the community forest. We have to do something, or the towns on Haida Gwaii aren't going to survive." Coming from John,

What's Growing? Wood Goods

Most of the markup, or "value added," is now at the consuming end of the Northwest economy—in frozen pizzas, not commodity wheat; computer tables, not Douglas-fir logs. Yet for a region that grows trees in such abundance, the Northwest produces astonishingly little wood furniture and other manufactured wood products. Specialized in commodity lumber and pulp, the region's timber economy is a classic example of a high-volume, low-value business. In British Columbia, running logs through a sawmill generates 2 jobs per million board feet. Average secondary wood processors in the province, making moldings and the like, can generate another 9 jobs from the same wood. Making furniture from a million board feet typically generates 80 jobs.[56]

Throughout this forested region, the value-added wood products business has been growing quickly in recent years, now employing 54,000 workers. Oregon and Washington lead British Columbia in value-added wood products, but the province has narrowed the gap. Its international exports have quadrupled every four years during the nineties. Still, British Columbia's steaming growth rate is only half Canada's. The province sends just one-tenth of its solid wood through the mill more than once, and it adds less value to that wood than other provinces.[57]

these words preempt any remaining hesitation. Only the Haida could block the plan at this point. Kim asks for volunteers to help prepare the proposal—a process that will undoubtedly consume scores of hours—and, one after another, most members of the board raise their hands.

THE COMMUNITIES OF Haida Gwaii make Ketchikan look like a boomtown. They are full of rot and mud. Compared with other places in the Pacific Northwest, the Queen Charlottes are dilapidated.

Yet they also have about them a tranquility that's increasingly rare. In Haida Gwaii, polarization is remarkably absent; the place offers a refreshing reprieve from the internecine warfare of Ketchikan and other Northwest towns. In Ketchikan, one friendly critic of the mill refused to give his name for fear of reprisals. "There's no possibility of rational discussion in town," he said. "The mill became a political litmus test."

In the Queen Charlottes, the process of forging a plan for the future has united an incongruous band of revolutionaries. Among them are not only the sovereignty-minded Haida but also a founder of the province's wise-use movement and the chair of the Sierra Club. If the entire Northwest could focus on its future the way Haida Gwaii has, with the sense of limits that islands impose, perhaps the entire Northwest would share its singularity of purpose. And perhaps more northwesterners would, as ICSI wrote in its blueprint, see "an ideal economy as one which generates greater social benefits at all levels from the use of fewer resources."

H A Y F O R K

Restoring the Watershed

SIX YEARS HAVE PASSED SINCE THE SPEECH AT A high school career day that changed Lynn Jungwirth's life and helped turn the town of Hayfork, California, into a laboratory for workforce conversion. Lynn was invited to class that day to tell the students about jobs she had held; she left with a mission. Of the 23 seniors, 17 had no idea what they would do after graduation. "Five wanted to stay in school another year," she says. "I went home and said to my husband, 'We just *have* to do something.'"

That was in 1992, shortly after a federal judge stopped all logging in the Trinity National Forest to protect the spotted owl. Hayfork's 18-year-olds figured the local economy was in its death throes. To Lynn and others her age—who had already weathered the long timber recession of the early eighties—things didn't look much better. "We realized that the jig was up," she says. "But we decided to take the scientists at their word and look into ecosystem management."

"With an optimism beyond reason," she continues, her eyes widening for emphasis, "we decided that the American people who had declared the spotted owl so important would surely continue to take care of the land." Whatever ecosystem management was, Lynn figured, somebody was going to have to *do* it. A restoration economy would require a versatile workforce with local knowledge and an attachment to place. Who better than the newly unemployed loggers?

So Lynn, a quietly irrepressible woman raised in a timber family in the mill town of Yoncalla, Oregon, launched a new community organization and a string of innovative projects. At the moment, on a January morning enveloped in pale light, she is describing her progress as we sit in the vacant variety store that serves as makeshift office for the Watershed Research and Training Center.

Training is the undisputed first priority for laid-off timber workers. A quarter of Oregon's unemployed loggers surveyed in 1990 were dropouts, and few of the remainder had any post–high school education. In the new economy, that's a résumé for poverty. So in 1994, the Watershed Center fielded its first training course, teaching a crew of idled lumberjacks how to clean up logging sites and replace fish-killing culverts. Each year the center, along with the local community college, state employment officials, and federal land managers, added features to the program: lectures on ecology, seminars on erosion control, practical sessions assessing wildlife habitat. From landscape surveys to computer mapping, emphasizing hands-on learning, the center imparted skills necessary for what Lynn calls an ecosystem workforce. Counties up and down the coast have emulated these courses.[58]

There is no shortage of work to do. The Trinity National Forest, like others, suffers from a sad history of too many roads and too few fires. The Pacific Northwest has half a million miles of eroding logging roads slung like spaghetti across its backcountry—enough road to loop around the equator 20 times. Closing, recontouring, and replanting enough of them to safeguard watersheds would generate thousands of jobs. Likewise, combating the spread of noxious weeds, restoring streams and wetlands, and cleaning up the gigantic hazardous waste sites at Washington's Hanford and Idaho's Silver Valley could keep a generation of northwesterners employed. At the same time, it could help return the land to a state of health and productivity unknown in decades.[59]

But no one has volunteered to pay for this Marshall Plan of ecological redemption. British Columbia's watershed program, the Northwest's largest initiative of first aid for nature, provided only 880 year-round jobs in 1998.[60]

HAYFORK IS IN California's appalachian zone. Hulks of rusting machinery surround homes. Giant trucks careen down roads, hauling away the remaining big logs from private timberlands. The topography is appalachian too. The valley surrounding Hayfork—a community of perhaps 1,800 people—is pinched by the ranges of the rugged Klamath knot, a mountainous tangle that extends from California's north coast into southern Oregon. The Klamath knot, cloaked in grass-floored woods of fir, pine, and oak, is, like Haida Gwaii, a global hotspot of species diversity.[61]

These mountains lack the broad valleys of the region's grander highlands, so crossing them is hard. Washboard ridges turn Hayfork into a town of extraordinary isolation, and isolation, unfortunately, brings poverty. Conventional wisdom among academic specialists has it that the principal obstacle to rural development in a global economy is "rurality"—which means, as best I can tell, being far from the action. Some 84 percent of students at Hayfork Elementary qualify for free or reduced-price lunches, says Lynn, up from 52 percent in 1989. The town's poverty rate is well above 30 percent.[62]

Trinity County is often labeled the most timber dependent in California, but the Watershed Center's research shows that what's good for timber interests is not necessarily good for local people. The poverty rate rose straight through a logging spree in the late eighties and kept rising in the bust that followed. "That was the most important thing the community learned from our research," Lynn says.

The all-time peak of the county's timber harvest was in the late 1950s, when the loggers were clearing the old growth. That early boom brought the Jungwirths to town for the first time. Lynn's husband Jim, who has joined us at the office, was then the ten-year-old son of a logger from Lebanon, Oregon. In those days, Jim says, the timber industry was local. Hayfork had seven mills, which gave the town both a diverse job base and a solid middle class of managers and millwrights. These people were the stalwarts of the village; they built the swimming pool, ran the Little League, and organized the volunteer fire department.

Timber reached a second peak before plunging into recession in the early eighties. That recession triggered deep restructuring: consolidation, downsizing, automation. In the spotted owl forests of California, Oregon, and Washington, the number of timber jobs per unit of timber produced decreased by one-quarter—and real payroll per unit of timber fell by one-third—between 1979 and 1989. By the time of logging's last hurrah in the late eighties, the diverse local industry had given way to one giant mill with absentee owners, and the community's capacity for leadership and entrepreneurship was, like the forests, depleted.[63]

The market was working, no doubt, orienting all minds toward maximizing profit. Hayfork was playing its part in the expansion of the gross national product; its part just happened to be small. Indeed, in the new economy overall, the division of labor seems to be that some specialize in winning and others—Hayfork among them—in losing.

True to form, in 1996, Hayfork lost its sawmill. Sierra Pacific closed it down and laid off 160 workers to further centralize its operations. Forty percent of Hayfork's payroll dollars disappeared. Poverty mounted. Methamphetamine abuse erupted. The condition of the housing stock, already bad, slid toward derelict. The local laundromat went bankrupt, leaving the poor with no place to wash clothes. Still, many hard-hit families stayed, piecing together livelihoods. "'Multiple income strategies' is what the employment agents call it," Lynn says. "But it's just doing anything you can."[64]

THE TRENDS IN family incomes in Hayfork since the fifties reflect larger shifts throughout the Pacific Northwest. The third quarter of the twentieth century was a period of middle-class expansion, when the income profile of the region's households resembled a diamond. A relative few were at the top. A matching few were at the bottom. Most were in the middle. During the century's fourth quarter, the diamond came to look more like an hourglass.

For the first time in its history, the region became a global launching pad for stratospheric wealth: by early 1998, it was home to the planet's first-, sixth-, and fifteenth-richest humans, along with three of the world's other 227 billionaires. Meanwhile, perhaps a quarter-million Northwest households had enough wealth to qualify as run-of-the-mill millionaires. In the United States overall, the richest 1 percent of families own 39 percent of all private assets. No comparable data exist for the Pacific Northwest, but the concentration of wealth is almost certainly greater. The top 1 percent of Northwest families likely own about half the region's private wealth. All by themselves, the Northwest's six billionaires controlled $96 billion in early 1998—more than the bottom two-thirds of households in the region put together. By early 1999, they controlled more than $150 billion, which is roughly one-tenth of all private wealth in the Pacific Northwest.[65]

But the new stratification is more than just the simple concentration of wealth in the hands of the superaffluent. At almost every level of the Pacific Northwest's class structure, economic trends have amplified inequality, augmenting rewards for the fortunate and heaping further misfortune on the unfortunate. In the Northwest states, for example, the top fifth of families with children increased their real average annual earnings from $90,000 in the late seventies to $107,000 in the mid-nineties. Average incomes for the poorest fifth of families with children, meanwhile, decreased from $12,000 to $10,000. So did average incomes for families with children in the middle fifth of the economic ladder, from $43,000 to $40,000. And these figures likely understate both the size and the growth of the income gap because they do not cover all forms of income.[66]

Similarly, real hourly wages for most workers were lower in the late nineties than they were two decades earlier. In 1979, workers halfway up the pay scale in the Northwest states made roughly $12.90 an hour; in 1997, similar workers made $11.50. Workers at the bottom of the pay scale—those in the 20th percentile—suffered proportionately larger pay erosion, dropping from an average wage of $8.20 to $7.00 over the same period. Those at the top of the scale, of course, flourished. In 1965, American CEOs got 20 times more in their pay envelopes than typical workers; by 1997, they got 116 times more.[67]

In Canada, similar trends unfolded. From 1981 to 1995, the lowest-paid tenth of male workers suffered a one-third cut in pay after inflation, while high earners saw comparable raises. In the early seventies, the top tenth of Canadian families with children made 21 times more than the poorest tenth; by 1996, they earned 314 times more. Partly to offset the slumping earnings of their husbands, women dramatically increased their hours of paid work, bringing home far more income than before. In the United States, too, women streamed into the workforce, their earnings helping to stave off poverty for the working class. High-income women also joined the labor force, redoubling the growth in cash flow to affluent families.[68]

In this sea of bad news about income distribution, there are at least two good tidings. First, British Columbia successfully dampened the impact of widening disparities in earnings through progressive taxes and government programs until 1994, although some evidence suggests that after-tax income disparities have widened in subsequent years. Second, income disparities widened more slowly during the nineties than during the eighties, and they may even have begun to contract after 1995 in the Northwest states. In the United States overall, wages increased relatively quickly from 1996 to mid-1998 for most workers, and the increases were largest at the bottom of the scale. Wages at the bottom of the scale ticked upward in Washington in the early and mid-nineties, too, modestly improving income distribution in that state. In fact, unlike Idaho, Oregon, and British Columbia, Washington saw income distribution become somewhat more equitable from the mid-eighties to the mid-nineties, partially reversing the marked deterioration between the late seventies and the mid-eighties. Extremely low unemployment rates appear to have helped boost the earnings of bottom-end workers.[69]

Roger Jaegel, a retired Forest Service lifer who grew up in Hayfork and now runs its training program for idled loggers, is at the site of the closed Hayfork mill, part of which the Watershed Center leases. "This is the Hayfork yarder," he says, proudly walking around a trailer-mounted piece of machinery that's the size of a camper. "Local folks developed it. We needed equipment that was small, versatile, and affordable." The yarder is designed to pluck tiny logs out of overstocked, fire-prone forests without marring soil or trees. Under a nearby shed roof stand two more big machines, waiting for winter to end. "All the small-diameter logs we take go through these," says Roger. "We cut them into boards or peel them for poles." The goal, Lynn adds, is to help finance forest care by selling its by-products. "We need the urban marketplace to pay for this work."

The biggest dilemma for depressed towns such as Hayfork—communities "trying to build a bootstrap to pull up on," as Lynn says—is that while the economy now requires extra education, spending local resources on training may squander funds on workers who leave immediately afterward. Most job opportunities are elsewhere, after all, and mobility rises with educational attainment.[70]

Lynn's course has been doubly successful, then, because it has drawn national and state funding *and* it has allowed trainees to stay in town. They have landed seasonal work using some of their new skills, but none of the 50 graduates have been able to create a full-time, year-round career in ecosystem care. The Forest Service has been slow to begin work on ecosystem restoration, and it has put the contracts out for bid the old-fashioned way: as specialized assignments across huge expanses of terrain. Center graduates can hardly bid on these jobs, lacking the access to financing and large pools of workers to compete with urban-based companies that hire migrant crews. Trinity County workers get only 7 percent of local Forest Service contract work. "The forest restoration work is all going to companies on the I-5 corridor," observes Lynn.[71]

So the Watershed Center has nudged the Forest Service to create new ways of bundling work. Called stewardship contracting, the idea is to organize bids by place rather than task. For instance, a Hayfork crew might do stream bank revegetation in the fall, mapping and monitoring in the winter, timber thinning in the spring, and road removal in the summer. A flexible bidding system would let workers integrate subsistence hunting and commercial gathering into their livelihoods. The gathering of wild mushrooms, floral greens, and medicinal herbs in the Pacific Northwest employs more than 15,000 people, many of them recent immigrants. One Watershed Center pilot project found that fast, knowledgeable workers could earn $20 an hour gathering mullein, a weedy alien plant that natural medicine practitioners use to treat respiratory problems.[72]

Any week now, the Forest Service will put its first stewardship contract out for bid. In the current forest economy, migrant laborers do the tree planting. Migrant helicopter crews do the logging. Itinerant specialists from the Bay Area do the surveys. Forest Service supervisors come on three-year rotations. Ecosystem management could fall into the same pattern, which is what scares Lynn. "Specialized crews won't ever be able to do good stewardship," she says. They don't have to live with their handiwork. To Lynn, the present pattern is the antithesis of community: "It isn't a viable economy if Dad is never home."

EDUCATION PLAYS A central role in the new inequality, but not because workers are less schooled. On the contrary, the share of workers in British Columbia with a university degree or some other postsecondary diploma rose from 40 percent in 1990 to 50 percent only six years later. In the United States, the share of workers who were high school dropouts fell from 36 percent to 13 percent between 1970 and 1991.[73]

Rather, education matters more than it once did, amplifying the extremes in earnings. During the seventies and eighties, occupations requiring the most education—professional, managerial, and technical—proliferated, expanding from 21 percent to 30 percent of all employment in the United

States. In British Columbia, more than half of all jobs created in the early and mid-nineties were managerial and professional positions.[74]

Just as university graduates—roughly the top quarter of the workforce—have gained the most, those with little education have suffered the most. Automation and overseas factories have largely displaced high-paying production jobs that required unskilled workers to repeat simple tasks. Other low-skill jobs have opened up, but they come with low pay. Unskilled workers in past generations could usually find high-wage jobs at the other end of a Greyhound bus trip; now they have to learn a trade.[75]

What is behind the bifurcation in northwesterners' earnings? The causes form a tangled knot, interlocking in ways nobody fully understands. But at least five factors are probably responsible.

First, rapid technical change such as computerization has put a premium on specialized skills. Putting a computer on every desktop, and a computer chip in almost everything else, has reordered not only the workplace but also payday; it has turbocharged the earning power of elite workers and replaced low-skill laborers in all sectors of the economy. Many economists blame technological change for most of the increase in income inequality, but in the Northwest, this theory is difficult to reconcile with recent trends. Washington State, for example, has had rampaging growth in high-tech industries since the late eighties, but its income gaps have narrowed somewhat over the same period.[76]

Second, high rates of legal and illegal immigration have driven down wages by expanding the labor pool. As much as 45 percent of the decline in earnings for high school dropouts in the United States in recent decades has come from this job competition.[77]

Third, swift globalization through international trade has driven cost cutting throughout the North American economy. In the United States, increasing trade probably accounts for between 10 and 30 percent of the increase in income inequality. But in the Northwest, the effects are likely smaller because of the region's unusual concentration of successful exporters.[78]

Fourth, the decline of unions has weakened labor's bargaining position, expanding income gaps. As jobs have moved out of manufacturing and away from regular, full-time employment, union membership has flagged. Unions represented 28 percent of employees in the Northwest states in 1983, but only 23 percent a decade later; in British Columbia, unionization dropped from 55 percent in 1958 to 37 percent in 1997.[79]

Fifth, the minimum wage has fallen behind inflation since the seventies, despite increases during the nineties in the United States overall and in Washington, Oregon, and British Columbia independently. In 1997, one-quarter of employees in the Northwest states earned less than $7.79 an hour—the wage a full-time, year-round worker needs to support a family of four above the U.S. federal poverty line. (And that poverty measure is the stingiest in the industrial world. A family of four at the U.S. poverty line has a monthly housing budget of $300 and a food budget of 63 cents per meal per person.)[80]

Whatever the causes of widening income gaps, the cures may not follow from the causes. Slowing the pace of technological change, for example, might help with inequality, but at a high cost to prosperity. Raising minimum wages modestly and indexing them to inflation would help the lowest-income workers, but if raised too high, minimum wages can do more harm than good. Similarly, moderating the pace of international immigration may make sense, but closing international borders entirely would violate an admirable humanitarian tradition. International trade rules more favorable to workers and the environment would help, but generalized protectionism is too indiscriminate a tool.

Closing the income gaps that have opened in the past 20 years may require broader public policies, such as tax reforms that favor workers, better public schools, and universal access

Organizing Service Workers

By convention, economists lump together as "service industries" all companies that do not produce tangible products. (Once, when producers of goods dominated the economy, this practice made sense. Now most of the economy provides services, and the old scheme obscures more than it clarifies. The business services category, for example, encompasses both janitors and management consultants.) As the service industries have grown, unions have begun to focus on organizing them—a challenge because service employees, unlike those in manufacturing, rarely work together in large numbers.

Organizing the service economy, from child-care centers to photocopying stores, is the new frontier for the labor movement. The Canadian Auto Workers (CAW) have organized low-wage, part-time employees at such retail chains as Chapters Bookstores, The Gap, and Starbucks. They have even organized a McDonald's restaurant in Squamish, B.C., an old timber town that now depends more on the tourist traffic heading past for the ski resort at Whistler. "It's the first McDonald's in North America to unionize," says CAW's Roger Crowther, who helped in the campaign.

to advanced education. And because the soaring investment income of the affluent is a principal cause of expanding disparities, it might also require public programs that enable working-class households to gain major assets such as homes and stocks.[81]

One thing is certain. Loosening environmental controls—to speed the timber harvest, for example—would provide no long-term benefit to low-income families. Hayfork's experience demonstrates that.

ROGER JAEGEL POINTS to patches of forest that have burned in recent years as he drives his pickup on a rutted dirt road to a site he calls "Chopsticks." For decades, the Forest Service suppressed fires, and small trees grew in dense thickets. The original forests of the area were parklike stands of widely spaced trees; the understory burned every year or two. "The

WEALTH, NOT INCOME

Investment income and other payments unrelated to work account for more than one-third of personal income in the Pacific Northwest, up from one-fourth in 1970. Global competition has squeezed wages and other business costs, creating both higher profits and widening social gaps. The owners of the more profitable companies have benefited in the form of rising stock prices. Middle-class households, for their part, at least benefit from their homes' rising real estate values. But blue-collar families, owning nothing that appreciates over time, fall further behind. This trend suggests a need for strategies, such as employee stock ownership plans, that help all workers to accumulate assets.[82]

ecology of this area, it wants to burn," Roger says. The same is true in huge swaths of the dry interior Northwest. Forests that have seen too much grazing and logging and too little burning have become tinderboxes. When fires burn now, they destroy rather than replenish the stand of trees. If left alone, these forests might eventually find their way to old-growth structure, but it might take several generations of catastrophic fires that endanger settlements.

Lynn and Roger walk through a glade different from others on this slope. Here, the center's crews used the Hayfork yarder to pluck out the skinniest trees—the chopsticks. Afterward, they burned wood that had accumulated on the forest floor. Selective thinning and prescribed burns can speed the return to an open forest by resetting the fire cycle.

"Our job in the Trinity forest is to create old growth," says Lynn. "We're just trying to figure out how."

BACK IN TOWN, Jim Jungwirth is putting finishing touches on a new set of retail shelves. Two years ago, inspired by his wife's efforts, he started a furniture and flooring company. The shelf, which he designed over the weekend, is for an Oregon chain that wants to better display smoked Alaska salmon. The prototype is made of blocks of alder (a tree that loggers once considered a weed) glued into boards. Piled nearby are samples of floorboards made of chopstick logs, ready for interested buyers in Seattle. Other merchandise crowds the impromptu factory.

With six employees and one partner, Jim is already a major economic force in town. His workers earn as little as $7 an hour, but he has turned a profit each year. The toughest part of his business, as for every value-added forest product maker in the rural Northwest, is marketing. He spends a lot of time in cities drumming up business.

In Trinity County, the timber industry adds little value to local logs, employing only slightly more people per unit of wood than on Haida Gwaii. Yet Hayfork has parts of a bootstrap built: turning skinny trees into furniture, gathering

JOBS AND TAXES

All spending, whether government or private, creates jobs; it just creates different jobs, in different places, for different people. But when government expands, it can cause more harm than good: in the process of creating public-sector jobs, it can destroy a larger number of private jobs by taxing away the funds that support the private sector or bidding up the interest rate that finances it. Government spending is a plus for all jobs when the funds go to efforts that help the economy work better overall—by enhancing the productivity of the workforce, by expanding basic research knowledge, by creating the means for more efficient transportation and communication, by reducing losses to crime and corruption, and by improving the quality of life that holds productive workers in place.

But how government raises money matters just as much as how it spends money. And at present, tax codes in the Northwest discourage work and promote resource depletion. Shifting taxes off paychecks and onto pollution is one way to boost employment, raise wages, benefit human health, and improve environmental quality all at once. A comprehensive tax shift in the region would expand the economy by an estimated 2 percent, even while curtailing harmful emissions and habitat disruption.[83]

forest herbs, contracting stewardship services. Unfortunately, the plan won't employ many ecosystem management technicians without a much broader program than what's in the offing. The barrier is funding.

"A commodity trickle will provide some funds," Lynn says, referring to Roger Jaegel's chopsticks logging. Restoration plans for endangered wild salmon will likely make some government funds available too. Government funds aren't to be sneered at; the public sector provided one job in eight in the Northwest in 1997. Most of these jobs, belying myths of bloated national governments, were at the local, state, or provincial level. Further belying myths of fast-growing governments at all levels is the fact that government jobs have increased much more slowly than the workforce overall. Since 1970 in the Pacific Northwest, government jobs have accounted for a declining share of all employment and of all personal income.[84]

But Lynn's long-term goal is to tap the richer, downstream beneficiaries of services provided by the Klamath knot. California reroutes much of the flow of the Trinity River eastward through a tunnel and dam to farm fields far to the south. Southern California wants more water, so upstream counties may be able to negotiate funds for restoration. "Millions of dollars worth of water and power flow out of this county every year," Lynn reasons. "We need something back to care for the sponge."

B O O N V I L L E

Tapping the Conservation Market

LAURIE WAYBURN IS POINTING OUT A FEW OF THE old redwoods of the Anderson Valley. From her vantage point in a small car on a winding state highway, most of what she can see is tidy vineyards, runty trees, and cow-burnt pastures. But here and there, jutting above this hobbit landscape, stand the awesome patriarchs—trees that were already taller than a cathedral in 1580, when Sir Francis Drake pirated up the coast to Oregon.

If you know where to go, Laurie is saying, you can walk among these living megaliths and imagine what the original Northwest must have been like, home to the heaviest accumulation of living matter on Earth. The temperate rain forests of the Pacific Northwest are better than any other ecosystem at absorbing carbon dioxide. "They are the best carbon sinks in the world," asserts Laurie.

Northwest rain forests store twice as much carbon per acre, on average, as tropical rain forests. Growing the Northwest's forests bigger, even if not to their original scale, would help slow climate change. Along the way, it would help dozens of imperiled species, stabilize watersheds, and enhance the region's quality of life.[85]

What she is up to, Laurie says, is transforming climate stabilization into a marketable product so that private landowners can earn money by letting their trees stand. A fifth-generation Californian who did conservation work in Africa and Latin America before returning home in the late eighties, Laurie founded the Pacific Forest Trust in 1993. The trust's mission is to preserve private forestlands in northern California, Oregon, and Washington, mostly through legal easements. These easements usually ban development and specify forest practices such as long rotations, wide stream buffers, and few roads. Private Northwest forests, because they are mostly on productive low-elevation sites, grow bigger and faster than public forests.

Eventually, carbon storage may be a market worth half a billion dollars a year in the rural Northwest. At the moment, however, Laurie is simply struggling to put a few deals together to tap the conservation market. In these deals, sellers—two have already signed contracts—receive money and agree to manage their forests to soak up carbon. Buyers—Laurie is negotiating with a handful of interested corporations—pay money to sellers and take credit for the carbon storage.

This January morning her quest is taking her a few miles down the Anderson Valley from her hometown of Boonville, California, to visit a beat-up timber tract newly bought by the Mendocino Redwood Company. The company is the third seller of a carbon easement with whom Laurie has worked. This valley, like the rest of the region, is hitching its wagon to services (here, tourism and retirement) and high-value, low-volume products (here, wine). Decades ago, the valley had 16 lumber mills; now it has 2.

KAREN MULLHAIR, A forester from southern California, stops her pickup on a steep road. Letting her Labrador retriever out of the back, she and Laurie talk about the stand of trees around them. "This is one of our better ones," Karen says. The trunks are larger, with fewer of the lower-value tanoak trees that thrive on overlogged hills.

"With a carbon easement, we could probably double the timber volume," Laurie suggests. Karen nods. Managing for carbon storage would lengthen the rotation and allow more selective cutting.

Karen's employer used to be forestry giant Louisiana Pacific, owner of Ketchikan's closed mill. But last summer, Louisiana Pacific sold its 200,000 acres of Mendocino woodlands to the newly formed Mendocino Redwood Company. Mendocino Redwoods has the cash to shake up business in forestry. It also has reason: television shots of industrial clearcuts in California's wine country might hurt sales at its owner's other business, The Gap clothing chain.

Farther up the road, Karen describes her efforts to safeguard streams and minimize damage from roads. "The roads have the biggest impact," she says. "With carbon's help, we think we can pay for the tanoak thinning, stretch our cut, and get a better quality of wood." They'll be cutting older, clear-grained trees, which command a premium.

Northwest forests actually grow more wood in their second half century than in their first, but the mathematics of compound interest augur against such long rotations. What foresters call the "economic age of rotation"—the age to which trees should grow to maximize profit—has been declining for years. "Forty years ago, it was an 80-year rotation," says Laurie. "Now it's down to 40." The trees themselves, meanwhile, only slow their growth at 120 to 200 years.

Carbon easements offer cash up front—effectively, a bribe to let trees stand—which better aligns forestry economics with forest growth. Fortuitously, protecting the Northwest's carbon banks will also help guard watersheds and fish and other wildlife, because streamside zones are the keys to all three.

To date, the potential buyers of carbon storage easements are major energy and chemical companies that emit huge volumes of greenhouse gases; they are participating in a voluntary federal program that records emissions reductions. But sooner or later, North American governments are likely to mandate action against climate change, and carbon storage credits will probably count toward complying with the law. Then the Forest Trust's easements are likely to become hot commodities—an exploding revenue stream to fund forest restoration.

ACROSS A MOUNTAIN range eastward from Boonville, a company taps the conservation market in another way.

David Fissel, the ponytailed operations director of catalog retailer Real Goods, has been with the company for a decade, making him an old-timer in a company whose workforce has grown tenfold—and whose revenue has grown a thousandfold—in ten years. "We've become an international business in a rural county," David says.

WHAT'S GROWING? CONSERVATION

An estimated 80,000 northwesterners work in companies whose bread and butter is environmental protection: hazardous and solid waste recyclers and managers, pollution control and prevention specialists, renewable energy generators, water and power conservers, environmental consultants and engineers. This sector grew extremely quickly in the late eighties, outpacing even health care, though its growth slowed somewhat in the nineties.[86]

Yet the true scope of the environmental workforce is larger. Big companies have environmental staffs of their own, and many firms integrate resource conservation into their operations, making it a responsibility of all workers. Moreover, whole sectors of the economy that are not explicitly environmental provide goods and services that further resource thrift and land conservation. The bicycling industry, public transit providers, and intercity bus and rail lines—plus those who build the infrastructure for them—offer alternatives to driving and flying. Repair and rental shops, secondhand stores, libraries, building renovation contractors, and urban redevelopers are the bulwark of reuse in an age that favors disposability. Software, information, and Internet companies hold up the hope of a paperless society someday. Health, exercise, educational, and cultural centers offer people nonmaterial rewards. And pathbreaking companies in every industry—from the proliferating number of organic farmers in the Northwest to the region's expanding guild of green builders—are offering wares brought to market in ways that set new standards for environmental responsibility.

A rare backwoods entry in the registry of overnight success stories in the Pacific Northwest, Real Goods is the world's leading retailer of solar power systems, household conservation gear, and other products for sustainable living. With 100 year-round employees, and twice as many during the holidays, Real Goods exemplifies the new economy: green, fast-growing, entrepreneurial, global, information intensive, stock financed, and low wage.

The world headquarters of Real Goods is a nondescript slab of cheap corporate real estate sandwiched between the Rancho del Ray Mobile Home Park and the Senior Plaza in Ukiah, California, a struggling town of 15,000 in the flat-bottomed valley of the Russian River. The only thing that distinguishes the building's exterior is the electric car–recharging station at its flank. But inside, the feeling is anything but corporate. Dozens of crowded cubicles decorated with political posters give the shop the feel of a campaign, which, in a way, it is.

In the mid-eighties, working out of his garage (the office space of choice for Northwest startups), founder John Schaeffer mailed a crude flyer to everybody whose address he could scrounge up, promoting renewable energy. He was soon selling solar cells and rechargeable batteries to deep-green consumers across the continent.

In the Real Goods call center, Janet Cannella is chatting with a customer about the merits of living off "the grid." She relies on a solar electric system herself, and she "loves to talk with people," which makes her a perfect employee. Janet has worked the phones here for four years, talking thousands of North Americans through their purchases of low-flow showerheads and compact fluorescent lightbulbs. Unlike some of the other seven people on duty this afternoon, Janet earns more than the starting wage of $7 an hour. And unlike the many part-timers on the phone banks, she gets medical and dental insurance. "It's a great job," she says, compared with her past work as an assistant in a dental office. Still, she won't have much to supplement her Social Security checks in a decade when it's time to retire.

For the company as a whole, David says, the largest challenge is that Ukiah does not have enough of the skilled, educated professionals that Real Goods needs to compete in the fierce mail-order market. Compared with big cities, the town offers stunning beauty, no traffic jams, and a low crime rate—qualities that draw retirees in droves. But managers recruited to take the company's top jobs tend to leave quickly.

So the company recently announced plans to move its executive offices an hour south to Santa Rosa, at the edge of the 6-million-person universe of greater San Francisco. The decision has been painful for the company. Human resources manager Helen Sizemore, a longtime resident, says, "Real Goods has been proud to be in Ukiah, and Ukiah has been proud to have Real Goods." Now, Real Goods is contributing to—or bowing to the reality of—the rural brain drain.

DEBBIE BANTA, A second-generation resident of Ukiah, has filled orders at Real Goods' warehouse for five years. Olive-skinned and strong-backed, she scales ladders to pick merchandise off shelves packed 20 feet high, earning $8.50 an hour plus health insurance. To get by on her pay, she lives with her mother. Her 22-year-old son works in the warehouse too.

Not many of Real Goods' employees ever worked in Ukiah's dwindling lumber mills. Most seem to be refugees from big cities farther south. But because Real Goods' Christmas hiring boom coincides with the slow season on the valley's pear orchards, many young workers go back and forth between packing pears and packing green goods.

A DOZEN MILES south of Ukiah on U.S. 101, called the Redwood Highway in this part of California, is the public face of Real Goods. Here, in the township of Hopland, company founder John Schaeffer has built a peculiar roadside attraction and inserted a retail outlet into it as the company's flagship store. Hopland, a vineyard town along a gurgling river in a mountain valley under a radiant sky, looks as if it might be the place where the range of Californian sun worshipers overlaps with the range of northwestern salmon worshipers.

Real Goods is perhaps the best-known name in the Northwest's alternative energy nexus. But there are hundreds of others. The most efficient refrigerators in the world are made in Arcata, California. One-fifth of the world's silicon crystals, used in photovoltaic cells, come from Vancouver, Washington. Some 274 companies plow the fields of renewable energy and energy efficiency in Washington State alone.[87]

Schaeffer, a bear of a man with a slow fire in his eye, walks the grounds and talks about the new economy. He is among the Northwest's great promoters but, paradoxically, comes across as almost shy. His Solar Living Center, by contrast, is outspoken. Every dimension of its construction and design springs from principles of environmental harmony—from the building materials (bales of straw) to the site layout (Stonehenge-style markers for each solstice). And almost every feature is explained on interpretive signs or on regularly scheduled tours. Part radical science museum and part medieval fair, the center embodies Real Goods' missionary business style. "Our goal is to convert the world from a fossil-fuel economy to a solar economy," explains John.[88]

The 12-acre complex of passive solar buildings, sun-pumped fountains and ponds, and organic gardens—all built on a restored waste dump beside the town's sewage treatment plant—attracts more than 100,000 motorists a year. They arrive curious and road weary, and most of them leave lighter in both wallet and heart. They have seen an Earth-friendly way of life that is, if whimsical, also technologically sophisticated; materially comfortable; and, in its spare way, beautiful.

What John is discussing, however, is not the $3 million center itself. He is talking about how, in the absence of enthusiasm from banks, he paid for it. "For most of the last decade," he says, "we've been a successful nonprofit business." Costs have grown as fast as revenues. In 1991, Real Goods did one of the first direct public stock offerings ever, selling stock straight to customers. It raised $1 million in eight months. Two years later, the company raised $3.6 million in four months through an offering that built the Solar Living Center. A third stock offering is now paying for the costs of opening a dozen retail stores, each in a different city.

The success of these stock offerings is difficult to explain on conventional grounds. They have raised millions of dollars from investor-customers all over North America—nearly 10,000 of them—despite a mediocre profit record. "Our shareholders have been extraordinarily patient with us," John says. Either they consider their stock ownership a charitable act, or they are gambling that the company will, by continuing to dominate the green goods market, be positioned to rake in large profits when some future day of reckoning comes.

Sooner or later, the investors may believe, the laws of nature will catch up with us, sending hordes of people scurrying to Real Goods.

Whatever the shareholders' motives, stock financing has been the key to Real Goods' growth—just as in the Northwest's other fast-rising sectors. Ballard, the Burnaby, B.C., developer of nonpolluting fuel cells that could replace internal combustion engines, rarely turns a profit on sales of its products. It makes payroll for its 563 employees with financing from investors and partners. Likewise, hundreds of Internet, biotechnology, and other startup companies that have yet to turn a profit are busily fueling the region's economy. They are pouring hundreds of millions of dollars into the region's common pot. Investors' beliefs about the future are critical determinants of what work gets done in the Pacific Northwest. Financing is a crucial but little-examined force in creating the new economy.[89]

Mail order, Real Goods' primary mode of operation, is wasteful, not conserving: putting 7 million catalogs in the mail every year tops the list of the company's eco-sins, which it confesses in painstaking detail in its annual reports. (To its credit, the company has jumped into tree-free Internet marketing with both feet, boosting Web sales 25-fold over the past year.) And the company's pay scale doesn't match that of Mendocino County's remnant timber industry. "Our company vision includes raising the telephone sales crews' pay to $10 an hour. That'd make it like choker setting."[90]

John knows about choker setting, the bottom job on the logging skill ladder. For a brief stint in the seventies, while still living on a commune, he labored in redwood logging camps. Now he faces a constant reminder. Across a stream from the Solar Living Center is a mill where rows of redwood four-by-fours, stacked taller than a man, wait to become new sundecks—a different kind of solar future.

The winds of economic change favor John's business, not the mill's. The only help he, or Laurie Wayburn, wants is an end to the subsidies that favor fossil-fuel energy and other unsustainable practices, along with stronger safeguards for nature. These reforms would expand the market for conservation—and make it easier to increase wages for Debbie Banta and Janet Cannella.

B E N D

Keeping the Money at Home

JOHN SCHUBERT'S NEMESIS LOOMS OVER NORTHEAST Second Street: a line of oil tanks standing four stories above Bend's industrial district. "This is where our gas and diesel come in," he says as he pedals across a stained refueling lot, his unassuming voice almost lost in the traffic noise. At the cabin office of American Pacific Petroleum, he inquires about the day's count.

"We expect five trucks and trailers today, straight from Portland," says the manager, a sunbaked old-timer with grease under his nails. Abbot Petroleum next door is pumping a tankerful of hydrocarbons into its storage silos. "Altogether," says John, "we probably burn 30 double rigs of petroleum a day here in Bend." Not far away, on Third Street, is John's other nemesis: Robberson Ford Mazda. At this hour, Rob Caudle's sales team is just getting started on selling the five new vehicles, mostly Ford pickups and sport utility vehicles, that they send off the lot on a typical day.

Paying for oil and cars sends millions of dollars out of the local economy each year, subtracting from the city's income and trimming its job count. Out of a dollar spent on gasoline, no more than 15 cents stays in Bend. The rest of the money disappears immediately to pay for drilling, transporting, and refining the fuel. Out of a dollar spent on a new car, at most a quarter stays in town.[91]

One strategy for local economic development is to plug the leaks—to replace major imports with local sources instead. The Northwest cannot drill its own oil or, in all likelihood, manufacture its own cars, but it can reduce its appetite for internal combustion by investing in alternatives to driving. Compact communities, pedestrian infrastructure, and public transit, therefore, are economic development strategies. Money that locals no longer need to spend on importing vehicles and fuel will be spent on other things. And a larger share of these nonautomotive expenditures will remain in the local area, circulating between residents and businesses. A million dollars spent on public transit, for example, generates five times as many local jobs as a million dollars spent on gasoline. So John Schubert's gas-saving crusade for Bend—the fastest-growing city in the Pacific Northwest in the nineties, and the largest city in western North America with no public transit—is also sound economic policy. "Trails and transit and better land use," he says. "Those are my issues."[92]

After eight years as a citizen activist and two years as an appointed planning commissioner, John decided to run for city council. Wiry, bearded, and balding, he is a tireless bicyclist whose friends occasionally have to remind him to unstrap his pant legs before beginning his campaign speeches. Today he is touring Bend by two-wheeler, chasing votes.

The challenge of taming auto and petroleum imports is not unique to Bend. The Pacific Northwest's leading imports from beyond its borders are motor vehicles and their fuel. The region spent more than $11 billion on new cars and trucks in 1998, plus more than $10 billion on petroleum. In the nineties, the region has earned less than $12 billion a year selling timber, wood, and paper. In fact, thanks to its relationship with motor vehicles, the Pacific Northwest is a net resource importer. In recent times, it has spent about $26 billion a year on oil, natural gas, and motor vehicles—the region's largest imports—while earning about $25 billion a year from sales of fish, minerals, and farm and forest products.[93]

JOHN PAUSES ON a bridge over the Deschutes River, which bisects Bend. "Upstream there, irrigation canals branch off from the river. Five of them radiate out through town. Alongside each is a ditch-rider road." John aims to convert the roads into urban trails to knit the community together. He and his allies have already won approval for a riverside trail the length of Bend.

Since 1990, John has been intent on releasing Bend from the full nelson in which the automobile holds it. The advocacy group for alternative transportation he assembled successfully pushed for bike-friendly policies and then widened its focus to include transit and community design. It convinced the city to paint bike lanes on streets, to improve sidewalks in areas of new development, to calm traffic and upgrade the pedestrian infrastructure downtown, and to enact what John regards as the best bicycle parking ordinance in the country. This law requires new developments to include bicycle racks and, in some cases, showers.

"We really brought bicycling into the consciousness of the community planners," he says as he turns onto a completed segment of the riverside trail, "and now it's a part of the landscape." Unfortunately, growing numbers of personal cars are part of the same landscape, and they have made the roads more menacing to pedestrians and cyclists despite the new sidewalks and bike lanes. John thinks a network of quiet trails would help, even as it linked city and countryside.

Beyond city limits, 2- to 20-acre ranchettes spread out for miles—farmland that sprouts more satellite dishes than profit-making crops. The operators raise horses, llamas, ostrichlike emus, and other curiosities, but every year since 1990, Deschutes County farmers have put more money into their husbandry than they have taken from it. For most of them, farming is a form of lifestyle consumption, not livelihood. (Of course, watering these lifestyle holdings drains the Deschutes of most of its summer flow as surely as did irrigating the production fields of the past.)[94]

Their situation is not unusual. On the majority of Northwest farms, farming is the second job rather than the first, ranked by income. Three-fourths of farm households in the Northwest states have off-farm earnings, and these earnings are substantial. In Washington they equal two-thirds of farm income; in Idaho, they exceed farm income; in Oregon, they dwarf farm income—five to one.[95]

"Only 30 years ago," John says, leaving the trail for a street downtown, "we were a timber town." Now the economy is driven by inbound migration of "retirees and younger people fleeing metropolises, bringing high-powered talent."

They come here for the natural resources, but not for the same ones that brought earlier settlers.

The resources Bend depends on now are its 250 annual days of sunshine and the federal lands, mostly open forests of juniper or Ponderosa pine, that occupy most of Deschutes County. These public lands—what local development officer Robin Roberts calls "enforced green space"—offer an almost embarrassing surfeit of recreational choices: dozens of wilderness lakes; thousands of miles of biking, hiking, horse, and snowmobile trails; hundreds of river miles of whitewater and fly fishing; 3,000 feet of vertical drop at the ski slopes on Mount Bachelor, west of town; and hundreds of feet of vertical rise on the climbing pitches of Smith Rock, north of town. When *American Demographics* magazine ranked the most

What's Growing? Outdoor Recreation

All of the Northwest is wild about outdoor recreation. The region's national and provincial parks attract more than 10 million visitors a year; wilderness visits, also measured in the millions, are growing by 5 percent yearly. There's an old joke among travel agents that outdoors lovers get to town in worn-out shorts with a $20 bill in their pockets and leave without changing either. Happily, the joke is out of date: recreation now generates spending, and jobs, in huge quantities. One credible study of the interior Columbia River basin pegged the recreation sector as accounting for 15 percent of all employment, more than twice the jobs in farming, mining, ranching, and timber combined. A different study tallied spending related to sportfishing, hunting, and wildlife watching at $1.4 billion in the Northwest states in 1996, more than two times the scale of these states' mining industries.[96]

livable small cities in America, Bend was 1 of 5 Northwest towns in the top 20. It's an urban pocket in a vast wilderness playground, and it's therefore a place in the thrall of the recreation cult. One sees a lot of Lycra.[97]

Bend's recreation cult made John's bicycling proposals a natural for the city, but transit is another story. The city has done nothing for transit besides a feasibility study. John and his allies won planning-commission support for a starter bus system, but the city council has so far remained unmoved.

Across the street from his largest campaign sign, John stops in front of a new coffee shop. The shopkeeper, as if to dare the city, has installed a bus stop and a bench at the curb out front. "Now," says John, "we're just waiting for the bus."

JOHN HAS FOLLOWED the river trail into an enormous construction zone, where earthmovers are reshaping a broad quarter of the city. "This is the old industrial part of town," he says, squinting against the sun. During the first half of this century, Bend had two of the biggest pine sawmills in the world, along with sundry other mills. By 1994, one particleboard plant remained. "The city approved a massive mixed-use development for this part of town. In many ways, it's a model of what Bend needs: city neighborhoods designed for walking."

The development is the brainchild of Bill Smith, a former mill manager turned developer, who has collected the real estate and designed what amounts to a second downtown for Bend. Conceived as an exemplar of the environmentally conscious "new urbanism" sweeping throught architecture and planning circles, the Mill District will convert a huge swath of riverfront property into a blend of offices, light industrial facilities, apartments, houses, shops, and public space.

Compared with conventional sprawl, urban zones of this type reduce driving by a third or more, which means more money will stay in the local economy and less pollution will go into the local air. (Bend needs help with its air; this morning, authorities issued a yellow alert for air quality.)[98]

Bend's skyrocketing fortunes are partly a product of the aging baby boom, according to Robert Raimondi of the Oregon Economic Development Department. Thousands of successful professionals confronting midlife crises in places they never really wanted to live, Raimondi says, "take their marbles and relocate, looking for a place with no bars on the windows." They pass through Bend and like what they see: natural amenities, a regional airport, and state-of-the-art telecommunications systems. More than 70 percent of Bend's current business owners first visited town for reasons other than business.[99]

The scale of amenity-driven relocation is poorly monitored. The best single study found that 2.4 percent of employed migrants to the state of Washington in the first half of the nineties were what regional economists call "lone eagles"—they worked alone from their homes, selling goods and services to distant markets. Another 6 percent of employed newcomers were telecommuters, typically working at home one-fourth of their days and traveling to their offices the remainder of the week. Both classes of workers have more education and money than other migrants: two-thirds are university graduates, and more than half enjoy at least $50,000 a year in household income. And these workers are just as likely as other employed in-migrants to move to rural places. If the same rates apply across the region, long-distance workers bring at least 500 high-wage jobs into the rural Northwest every year. Washington's lone eagles and telecommuters, many of whom are married to retirees, cite the natural environment and recreational opportunities as their primary reasons for choosing their new homes.[100]

The conversion of the Mill District is a fitting emblem for Bend's transition, now largely completed, from home of

What's Growing? High Tech

Conservatively estimated, the Pacific Northwest had more than 400,000 high-tech jobs in 1997; the resource industries had 308,000 jobs. And high-tech jobs such as those in aerospace, electronics, software, and biomedicine mostly pay well, averaging $52,000 a year.[102]

These businesses thrive around Puget Sound, which has become a world growth center for technology companies. A self-perpetuating cycle of innovation and entrepreneurship has taken hold in greater Seattle, generating new ventures at a rapid clip. More of Washington's employment is in high tech than any other state's, with aerospace the largest high-tech sector and biotech the fastest growing. By 1998 there were probably more programmers and other computer workers in Washington than there were loggers in the entire Northwest—and the software guild's earnings averaged an astonishing $140,000 a year.[103]

The high-tech economy has other concentrations, too, notably in the Willamette Valley and Boise. In Oregon, high-tech employment has grown at double-digit rates throughout the nineties, overtaking timber employment in 1995. British Columbia's high-tech sector has lagged but is catching up: jobs for computer specialists have been appearing ten times faster than other jobs during the nineties.[104]

hewers of wood to lifestyle hotspot in the global high-tech economy. Deschutes County's timber jobs have dwindled, falling behind construction jobs in 1994 and high-tech and other non-wood-manufacturing jobs two years later.[101]

Indeed, since 1979, the number of local high-tech jobs has climbed from almost none to more than 1,000. Workers

The electronics profusion is overhauling low-tech sectors of the economy too. Software and the Internet are replacing book and record stores; insurance, loan, and stock brokers; travel agents; tax preparers; and even, for tasks such as wills, lawyers. North Americans spend much more money on computers than on televisions. Even in rural parts of Washington State, 40 percent of households have personal computers; in greater Seattle, almost two-thirds of families do. In fact, American businesses allocate half of all the money they spend on durable goods to computer hardware. More and more, we are becoming an economy that consists of people sitting at computers, sending e-mail to one another.[105]

High-tech industries are much gentler to ecosystems than resource industries, but they have a way to go to harmonize their operations with nature. Manufacturing each computer chip in Oregon generates about 7 pounds of hazardous wastes and consumes about 2,300 gallons of water. Some high-tech industries may pollute relatively little or consume relatively few resources locally but have damaging impacts elsewhere. Making Boeing airplanes, for example, gobbles imported, energy-intensive aluminum by the boxcar, while finished Boeing airplanes, sold to airlines on six continents, emit about 1 percent of climate-changing carbon dioxide worldwide.[106]

in these positions make everything from specialized semiconductors to lightweight commuter aircraft, and they work in firms that are mostly small, mostly new, and mostly linked more closely to world markets than to local ones. The Mill District is the kind of environment in which such firms, and their workers, are likely to take up residence. Skilled workers like strong communities close to unspoiled nature.[107]

"THIS IS MY BEST precinct," John says as he makes a campaign swing through an old neighborhood close to downtown. "There are lots of these old mill cottages mixed with bigger houses. The managers and the laborers used to live side by side here, walking distance from the mill." One of John's top priorities for this neighborhood is to keep its elementary school open. The school district wants to close it and put the students in a large building on the edge of town, beyond walking distance.

In a way, it's an instance of the public sector copying the private. Wal-Mart and other big-box retailers have swept into Bend's periphery, undercutting local shops and taking markets from stores in outlying towns. The consolidation of retailing into regional hubs such as Bend has been one of the big changes in rural economies in the nineties. Laments John, "We're getting big-box schools to match our big-box stores."[108]

ONE OF JOHN'S paid jobs is at St. Charles Medical Center. (It's fitting; health care is among the region's growth sectors.) Outside its main entrance, he points across the parking lot to a helicopter landing pad: a blue-and-red chopper marked Air Life of Oregon sits on the tarmac, its blade still spinning.

"Alternatives to the car aren't just about the economy or the environment," he says. They're about saving lives. Car crashes killed 1,991 northwesterners in 1996 and injured thousands more. "I'll never forget the time one of the Air Life pilots sought me out after a speech. He said, 'What I've seen! I think we should just ban cars.' "[109]

IN THE OFFICIAL ledgers of Deschutes County income, "dividends, interest, and rent" ranks larger than any employment sector of the economy, with government transfer payments such as Social Security close behind. Between them, these nonlabor sources accounted for 38 percent of the county's total income in 1995. In the entire Northwest, fully 45 percent of the growth in total personal income since 1979 has come from nonlabor sources. Retirement dollars account for about half this growth, but the region attracts many younger wealthy people as well.[110]

John visits a place where some of them congregate, a gated golf course community called Broken Top. He has slipped past the gates and is eyeing the mansions tucked into clumps of pine. Many of the owners are "equity exiles," people who have sold an exorbitantly priced house elsewhere and, after buying one here, still have enough left over to make a generous nest egg. Others hold stock or own businesses elsewhere. "There are six gated communities in Bend now," notes John. They provide second homes for former governors and Nike executives and first homes for the local elite.

Unlike the mill managers housed among their employees, the winners in the new economy rarely even see the losers. Inside Broken Top, the closest thing to the working class today is a young man laying sod in the manicured median near the clubhouse. More northwesterners now work in landscaping than in ranching. The danger of the service economy is that, for many, it becomes a servant economy.[111]

Bend is attracting so many people who can afford to pay top dollar for real estate that young workers are getting clobbered. The value of residential lots in town has multiplied 12-fold in the past 25 years, and the housing squeeze has spawned the trailer courts and apartment blocks that spread in pockets on the urban fringe. One-tenth of the Northwest states' residents live in trailers. In British Columbia, 29 percent of households are overstretched by housing costs, spending more on housing than the 30 percent of income specialists recommend.[112]

The Pacific Northwest's affliction with supervalued real estate and scarce affordable housing is most obvious in ski resort towns such as Jackson Hole, Wyoming, and Sun Valley, Idaho—places where only millionaires can afford to buy a home, and many local workers commute each day from distant towns. But the phenomenon is evident throughout the region. Many Northwest communities have experienced double-digit growth rates in land values each year during the nineties. Even in most remnant timber towns, real estate has appreciated mightily—tripling every five years in places like Mill City and Sweet Home, Oregon. And although much of this bidding war is for first homes, it is augmented by affluent buyers acquiring second and third homes.[113]

Some 113,000 houses in the Northwest states are vacation homes, 3 percent of the total. That share has more than doubled since 1970 as the pace of second-home development has outpaced first-home development. In Deschutes County, as in 28 percent of Northwest counties, more than 10 percent of houses are second homes.[114]

Though they sit empty much of the year, these finely appointed ghost houses nonetheless bring money into the local economy. They unleash realtor commissions, property taxes, and checks to home-security services. Still, it's a strange kind of economy, one that can bring nostalgia for the days of big mills, a shared work life, and tangible products. But large forces are at work, and they are likely to bring more of the same: American baby boomers are just beginning to inherit the estimated $10 trillion their parents have accumulated. And some of them are going to want a house in places like Bend. Developers are projecting a doubling of the market for vacation homes in the United States in the decade ahead.[115]

All that construction takes its toll on the environment. The approximately 100,000 new residences the Northwest builds each year consume resources on an awesome scale. A typical new house contains roughly 150 tons of wood, metals, and other materials, about the same amount of stuff as its residents are likely to put out in the trash during the structure's 80-year life span. Construction accounts for 40 percent by weight of the raw materials consumed by the U.S. economy, and buildings use about 40 percent of the Northwest's energy. While most new homes are built to accommodate the region's swelling population, rural trophy homes—the ridgetop mansions that are cropping up across the region—are the champion consumers. Their inflated size increases their resource content, and their isolation boosts driving and road building. Development overruns an acre of rural land every nine minutes in the Northwest states, and sprawl fragments habitats tens of times larger. Aside from logging and farming, no activity disrupts the Northwest landscape as much as development.[116]

Today, in Bend, the most important thing happening to the local economy—floating as it does on a huge cushion of retirement and investment income—is transpiring in faraway financial capitals: a 1 percent drop in the Dow Jones index and a parallel dip in the Nikkei. The flickering disappearance of tens of billions of dollars from the world cuts into Bend's largest income stream, investments.

Of course, today's downturn is utterly unremarkable; markets always fluctuate. The important trend has been the sweeping rise of paper wealth in recent years. It has given many potential migrants enough net worth to move to rural hideaways. Capital gains—increases in prices of stocks and other assets—have grown fast with the bull market, doubling in Oregon from 1995 to 1997 alone. Of the $12 trillion value of the American stock market, some 90 percent belongs to one-tenth of households, so most capital gains flow to the richest Americans. In fact, fewer than 40 percent of North American households own any stock at all. The top 5 percent of American households now receive more than $50,000 a year, on average, in investment income. British Columbians get a larger share of their income from investments than the residents of any other Canadian province.[117]

AT A RECEPTION, John sees his friend Peter Geiser. A financial adviser whose clients include some of Bend's moneyed newcomers, Peter notes the other negative consequence of the arrival of big money in Bend. "People come here to simplify their lives and be close to nature, but because of where they're coming from, they don't even see what they're doing: the big homes, expensive cars, and other trappings. Among the people here 25 years ago, there wasn't the conspicuous consumption. Now it has come with a vengeance."

Call it "equiptionism" or a "gear fetish": outdoor recreation as practiced by many is an extension of the shopping mentality into the wilderness. But ecologically speaking, the manufacture and use of human-powered outdoor gear is of no greater (or lesser) consequence than northwesterners' consumption of human-powered indoor gear, such as clothing, home furnishings, and cosmetics. The impacts of these goods, traced backward along their global production lines and

The Work Pace

Like earnings, hours worked per person have polarized in the past quarter century. High-wage employees are putting in more hours than ever, while low-wage employees are seeing their workweek shrink as part-time positions with few fringe benefits proliferate. On both ends of this spectrum, workers are unhappy, suffering from too little time or too little money. Indeed, the time-poor talk about spending and saving hours the same way the money-poor talk about spending and saving dollars.

One strategy for narrowing income gaps while improving quality of life is to offer employees work arrangements that are more flexible. A four-day workweek, early retirement, sabbatical years, longer vacations, and prorated benefits for part-time work are all excellent options for time-starved workers, but public policies do not encourage firms to offer such options. With more options, we might see a more equal distribution of labor—and of the time to enjoy its rewards.[118]

aggregated over a burgeoning population, add up to an ecological colossus. Still, they do not match the impacts of motorized recreation and travel—and the motorized transportation that begins and ends most outdoor excursions.[119]

Personal watercraft (a.k.a. jet skis) and snowmobiles, at $6,000 apiece, cruise the region's waterways and backwoods by the tens of thousands. Noisy and dangerous, these sport vehicles pollute the air far more than the cars that tow them out of town. Other waterborne sport craft, too, leak oil and fuel into lakes, rivers, and bays. One hour of water-skiing typically pollutes more than 12 hours of driving. Off-road motorcycles and buggies add their share of insults to the Northwest's nature, polluting the air about 15 times as much in an hour as a car. On-road vehicles, though cleaner running, are an even larger problem because of their numbers.[120]

Northwesterners own more than 600,000 sport utility vehicles (SUVs) and buy close to 50,000 new ones each year. Some 11,600 new Ford Explorers; 7,500 new Ford Expeditions; and smaller numbers of new Cherokees, Blazers, and other four-by-fours hit the streets of the Northwest states in 1997, making up about 16 percent of all new cars sold. Scarcely one-tenth of SUVs ever go off the road at all; most merely migrate among home, work, and errands in their suburban habitat. The increased popularity of personal trucks, which burn 50 percent more gas per mile than typical cars, has wiped out much of the region's progress in other forms of energy conservation since 1985, boosting the region's gasoline appetite by about 5 percent over what it would have been had trucks not swept the market. Overall, more than half the new passenger vehicles sold in the Northwest are now SUVs, pickups, and minivans, and these and other trucks, which made up about a third of the region's vehicle fleet in the mid-eighties, are on track to outnumber cars by 2005.[121]

The ascendance of the SUV, however, does not mark the endpoint for gas-guzzling recreation in the Pacific Northwest. That honor is reserved for the motor home and its close relatives, the camper and the travel trailer. Lined up bumper to bumper, the half-million on-road recreational vehicles registered in the Northwest would stretch more than 2,500 miles—from Boonville to Ketchikan (or to Prince Rupert, B.C., where the ferry leaves for Ketchikan) and most of the way back to Vancouver, B.C. With swiftly rising sales and millions of baby boomers approaching their golden years, the RV industry is gearing up to be the next step for an SUV-crazed region.[122]

The growth of our appetite for motorized recreation is an example of rising high-end consumption patterns that threaten to overwhelm the environmental benefits of the region's job transition. We log somewhat fewer old-growth forests and mine fewer mountainsides, but we log more vehicle miles and pave more watersheds. And we are exporting a larger share of the negative impacts of our consumption, as globalization lets us buy the wares of six continents. Like other North Americans, northwesterners consume their body weight in natural resources every day. For all the world's people to consume at these rates, we would need four planets; in other words, we're three planets short.[123]

For two decades, technical improvements in resource efficiency and pollution prevention have poured out of engineering laboratories, spurred by new laws and social values. But bigger houses and cars, new gadgets, more trips, and all manner of other things have counteracted most of the new techniques. In the Northwest, environmental impacts per person have not grown, but they have declined little. In the region, per capita energy consumption and greenhouse gas emissions are high and stable; per capita water consumption (mostly for irrigation) is high and declining, as are per capita pollution of air and water and generation of toxic waste. Per capita solid waste generation is still rising, though recycling has slowed the increase in per capita solid waste dumping. (Aggregate impacts, of course, are mostly rising with population growth, and current rates are too high.) No regional figures are available for other measures of the economy's environmental impacts, but in the United States as a whole, per capita consumption of wood, metals, industrial minerals, paper, and construction materials is high and, with few exceptions, stable.[124]

The historic opportunity open to the Pacific Northwest is to capitalize on its strengths in low-impact industries without squandering the resulting affluence on Earth-wrecking consumerism. The Northwest could apply its high-tech tools to the challenge of shrinking the regional economy's ecological footprint by an order of magnitude, wedding paperless communications with sustainable lifestyles, for example, and zero-emissions vehicles with walkable communities. The danger, on the other hand, is that the Northwest will get rich selling cybernothings to the world and, having long since displaced its rural working class, proceed to turn the region's hinterlands into a monoculture of tastefully appointed second homes.[125]

The most difficult problem in reconciling work and nature, in other words, is not improving resource efficiency; it is developing a sense of sufficiency.

New Northwest

Choosing a Future

THE SUN HAS BACKLIT THE RAIN CLOUDS IN SEATTLE this March morning, but in Ketchikan and Haida Gwaii, it's still pitch black and the rain falls uninterrupted—globes of North Pacific moisture diving onto spruce needles. Perhaps it was this grave weather that inspired what many regard as North America's most magnificent native art: the totem poles and longhouses of the Northwest Coast peoples. The great Haida sculptor Bill Reid once tried to express what need these poles fulfilled:

> [A] story of little people, few in scattered numbers, in a huge dark world of enormous forests of absurdly large trees, and stormy coasts and wild waters beyond, where brief cool summers gave way forever to long black winters, and families round their fires, no matter how long their lineages, needed much assurance of their greatness.[126]

Social scientists have long known that the motivation to work is much more than a desire to maximize income. In addition to livelihood, work is about joining a community of labor and defining one's identity. It's about pride and self-respect, about providing assurances of our greatness. And the story of the honorable laborer, the person who works unmediated with nature to wrest true timber, fresh fish, and mineral ore from the Earth provided such assurances. It was dangerous work and produced tangible goods. It also produced a powerful mythology. Who could argue with the nobility of it, especially when compared with the ephemeral qualities of perfecting a $3 cup of coffee or creating a more memorable ad jingle?[127]

Yet the Northwest of logging camps and fishing crews, of mill whistles and rain falling into lunch buckets, is fast disappearing. The resource industries don't work that way anymore. They've up-skilled and downsized like all the others. Blu Davis's Northwest is not yet as gone as Bill Reid's, but it is nearly as gone. And the choices we northwesterners make are determining the shape of what replaces it.

This Saturday morning, my work is in the unpaid economy, replacing some broken molding in my family's rundown Seattle house. First I will go to a specialty shop in my neighborhood where the vivacious owner, Nancy, who has a commanding knowledge of this city's doorframes and baseboards, will help me pick out exactly the right strips of precision-cut second-growth hemlock to match the original woodwork. The house itself, built around 1910 and remodeled in the fifties, has solid old-growth beams behind the plaster walls. So the Northwest's century-long logging boom—which helped pay my father's way through college—built my home, along with many of the Northwest's towns and cities. But nowadays the region's timber industry is increasingly made up of urban, specialty wood makers: Nancy and her employees will keep most of the $1 per linear foot I will pay for my few ounces of perfectly proportioned hemlock. The logger who felled it will get pennies. I would happily pay more if I had the choice to buy wood similarly proportioned from a forest that was independently certified as sustainably managed, but to date, certified wood does not come in the right shape for my baseboards.

As I run a tape measure across the walls—"measure twice, cut once," carpenters say—my mind ranges over the towns I have visited. In the weeks since each visit, events have continued to unfold. In Haida Gwaii, the community forest proposal is awaiting approval from the provincial government. In Hayfork, forest stewardship contract bidding will begin any week now. In Boonville, Mendocino Redwoods is more enthusiastic than ever about selling carbon storage. In Bend, John Schubert is a city councilor, having won more votes than any other candidate.

I am heartened by their progress, though even their combined efforts are small in comparison with the enormity of the Northwest economy. Still, small need not mean insignificant. After all, the economy is nothing but the aggregation of millions of minuscule efforts. And hundreds of initiatives similar to those described in this book are under way across the Northwest, aiming to align work and nature.

WHAT CONCLUSION CAN residents of other rural towns reach from this book? How can they more gracefully navigate the decline of the extraction economy? Is the message that timber towns should turn themselves into tourist traps or destination resorts, making themselves beautiful places in hopes of attracting beautiful people? No. It is that rural places need to identify the real sources of their strength and nurture them. Sad to say, there are no panaceas, only lessons.

Extraction is rarely as important to local economies as residents believe. Indeed, Lynn Jungwirth and the people of Hayfork attest to the futility of banking on extraction. Rather, towns can nurture local leadership and build community solidarity, as have Kim Davidson and the people of Haida Gwaii. They can cultivate entrepreneurship: it's what put 100 year-round conservation jobs in an orchard-and-mill town like Ukiah. They can add value to local resources and, by improving transportation and land-use patterns, trim resource imports, as John Schubert is doing in Bend. Like Laurie Wayburn of Boonville, they can tap the conservation market in innovative ways.

Northwest towns can focus on permanent residents, not just tourists; on services, not just manufacturers; and on nonlabor income, not just earnings, because the economy is moving in these directions at high speed. Above all, towns can refuse to sacrifice environmental quality for jobs. Not only is that sacrifice a bad deal, but it won't work. The economy now rewards strong communities close to unspoiled nature, so the best way to bring jobs to your community is to make it a better place to live and do business.

All northwesterners, whether rural or urban, can support sustainable livelihoods with their purchases. They can also support public policies that fund ecosystem restoration on public lands, improve educational opportunities, trim subsidies to anti-environmental activities, and shift taxes from low-income workers to polluting and resource-depleting activities. But the key policy task is to establish the conditions in which the private sector can generate good jobs—not to generate them through government spending.

Provincial, state, and local governments that want to create jobs may do best to focus their attention on objectives beyond jobs: strong communities, clean and healthy environments, excellent schools and universities, an efficient public sector, and good infrastructure. By aiming for these objectives, they are more likely to get a high-wage, low-waste economy.

This strategy can be difficult to achieve politically, because politics is the business of making headline news. Economic development, on the other hand, rarely generates headlines. It's an inescapably incremental, evolutionary process of millions of almost invisible changes, stemming from the decisions of millions of people and from the actions of hundreds of thousands of businesses, government agencies, and nonprofit organizations. In the quest for headlines, politics seeks to create visible winners and invisible losers, not visible losers and invisible winners.

That's the trouble. To speed the reconciliation of jobs and environment, policymakers can slash subsidies to uneconomical, anti-environmental sectors. But doing so creates visible losers and invisible winners.

Just so, a wholesale greening of the tax code, stepped-up investment in education and worker retraining, programs that provide working-class families with a starter "stake" of wealth, high standards that protect the environment and human health, and assertive curbs on sprawl would all help economy and ecology at once, especially over the long run. But enacting these reforms is difficult because of the headlines problem: all are susceptible to the organized opposition of readily mobilized interests—loggers, minerals processors, and developers, for example—talking about the threat to jobs. The reforms would, in fact, strengthen the economy. The jobs sacrificed, however, are visible ones held by known local people, while the jobs to be created are prospective ones to be held by unknown people, possibly newcomers.

The natural dynamic of politics, therefore, favors programs that create visible jobs, by using subsidies to recruit or retain large corporations or by building high-profile public works such as highways. As means of job creation, such programs usually do more harm than good. Collecting the taxes to pay for them dampens the economy more than the spending stimulates it. So the challenge in the Northwest is to seize upon extraordinary moments in politics—as I write this, for example, the U.S. government has listed nine salmon runs in the Northwest states as threatened—and, in these moments of policy ferment, to push tenaciously for the needed reforms.

Ultimately, however, politics is but a projection of public will, blurred and distorted though it may be. So public will is the final arbiter of the jobs environment. More than all the stacks of research findings I've studied, visits to five towns have made me see this region as confronted with two starkly opposed options.

The Northwest can show the world how to combine the best of the new, some of which is for sale in Real Goods' catalog, with the best of the old, such as Jim Jungwirth's wooden furniture. We can match fuel cells with organic foods, industrial ecology with selective logging, and cell phones with a shorter workweek. We can create compact neighborhoods where automobiles are an accessory to life and not its organizing principle. We can foster a region of ecologically sound farms, fisheries, and forestry operations, which restore nature while generating livelihoods. We can demonstrate that prosperity need not be synonymous with excess. We can, while curtailing our emissions of greenhouse gases, revitalize our living space by nurturing older forests, restored rivers, and a regenerating landscape.

Or, by failing to act, we can allow the Pacific Northwest to become a thoroughly bifurcated society. One in which those who can afford the price of admission enjoy a lifestyle of unparalleled recreational opportunities: fishing lodges, ski chalets, and oceanfront resorts. And one in which those who cannot afford admission may be able to, well, buy a trailer of their own someday. If they fail to toe the line, there is always the prison system—the fastest-growing public-sector employer in the Northwest states.[128]

A new Northwest of mute-toned Range Rovers and stylish rural getaways may be prettier to look at than the old Northwest of mud-splattered log trucks and industrial clearcuts, but it's no more viable over the long term. Sooner or later, northwesterners will need to inform both their policies and their lifestyles with the kind of reverence for place that they espouse so convincingly in conversation. They will need to say, "We've got enough," and mean it.

The truth of the matter is, we choose our future every day through our actions. In the end, fostering a green-collar economy boils down to a few personal questions. Will we choose to harmonize work and nature? Will we choose sufficiency or excess? Will we choose one Northwest or two?

Acknowledgments

Northwest Environment Watch (NEW) thanks peer reviewers Fran Korten, Roslyn Kunin, Fiona MacPhail, Ernie Niemi, Ray Rasker, Gundars Rudzitis, Priscilla Salant, and Paul Sommers for their skilled contributions. For their dedicated assistance, we thank our interns Ken Baldwin, Joanna Lemly, Erika Swahn, and those listed on the title page and volunteers Lisa Gettings, David Huffaker, Russell Jones, Dana Klein, Norman Kunkel, Lyn McCollum, Ajitha Rao, Marilyn Roy, Jessica Sanders, and Suzy Whitehead.

NEW is grateful to its board of directors: Mae Burrows of Burnaby, British Columbia; Aaron Contorer and Jeff Hallberg of Kirkland, Washington; David Yaden of Lake Oswego, Oregon; Sandi Chamberlain of Manson's Landing, British Columbia; and John Atcheson, Alan Thein Durning, and Sandra Hernshaw of Seattle.

NEW appreciates the board of NEW BC, our sister Canadian organization: Mae Burrows, Sandi Chamberlain, and Alan Durning (of NEW's board) along with Rick Kool, Heather MacAndrew, and Donna Morton of Victoria and Cheeying Ho of Vancouver. We thank NEW BC interns Russell Buri, Dean Hardman, Sarah Howard, and Satara Malloch.

Financial support for this book was provided by the Brainerd and Ford Foundations and contributors to Northwest Environment Watch. These include more than 1,500 families and individuals; the C. S. Fund; Rachael and Aaron Contorer; the Merck Family Fund; and the Bullitt, Nathan Cummings, William and Flora Hewlett, Horizons, Henry P. Kendall, Lazar, True North, Turner, and Weeden Foundations. Financial support for NEW BC was provided by the Endswell Foundation.

The author thanks NEW's staff: Ellen W. Chu, editorial director; Rhea Connors, office manager and volunteer coordinator; Meg O'Leary, membership assistant; John C. Ryan, research director; and Steve Sullivan, membership director. He also thanks NEW BC's director, Donna Morton, and office manager, Amanda Pawlowski.

ALAN THEIN DURNING is founder and executive director of Northwest Environment Watch and author of *This Place on Earth* and *How Much Is Enough?* He lives with his wife and children in an old Seattle house with new molding.

N O T E S

1. Timber employment from Alaska Dept. of Labor, "Southeast Alaska Industry Employment, 1990–1998," *www.labor.state.ak.us/research/emp_ue,* Feb. 12, 1999, and ECO Northwest, "The Potential Economic Consequences of a Reduction in Timber Supply from the Tongass National Forest," Eugene, Ore., Dec. 1994.
2. Average earnings from Brad Knickerbocker, "Chainsaw Requiem," *Christian Science Monitor,* Sept. 24, 1996.
3. Throughout this book, total figures for the Pacific Northwest refer only to British Columbia, Idaho, Oregon, and Washington and exclude northwestern California, southeastern Alaska, and western Montana; these partial states are home to 1 million people (three-fourths of them in California) and roughly 600,000 jobs. Population from spreadsheets assembled by NEW using data from U.S. and Canadian censuses and other federal population estimates; most data from U.S. Bureau of the Census, *www.census.gov;* B.C. Stats, Ministry of Finance and Corporate Relations, Victoria; and Statistics Canada, Canadian Socio-Economic Information Management System Time Series Data Base (CANSIM), Ottawa. In following notes, these data referred to as "NEW population data." Northwest workers from Linda Coldwell, analyst, B.C.

Stats, Ministry of Finance and Corporate Relations, Victoria, private communication, Jan. 8, 1999; Jeff Hannum, state labor economist, Oregon Employment Dept., Salem, private communication, Jan. 20, 1999; Jon Wines, Labor Market Information Center, Washington Employment Security Dept., Olympia, private communication, Jan. 22, 1999; and Kenneth Lux, Oregon Employment Dept., Salem, private communication, Jan. 6, 1999. Northwest gross regional product, in 1996, from U.S. Bureau of Economic Analysis, *www.bea.doc.gov/bea/regional/gsp/gsplist.html,* early 1999, and B.C. Stats, "British Columbia Economic Accounts: Service and Goods Industry Accounts," *www.bcstats.gov.bc.ca* at "Subjects," "BC Economic Accounts," early 1999.

4. Remaining rain forest from ECO Northwest, op. cit. note 1.
5. Mill history from ECO Northwest, op. cit. note 1.
6. Mill trouble from David Whitney, "Pulp Mill Hangs in Balance," *Anchorage Daily News,* Jul. 10, 1996; Hal Bernton, "Showdown in Ketchikan," *Portland Oregonian,* Apr. 14, 1996; and Hal Bernton, "Pulp Gold: Alaska's Bitter Harvest," *Seattle Times,* Apr. 28, 1996.
7. Ketchikan appropriation and quotes from Whitney, op. cit. note 6. Forecasts from "Mill Closure Impacts Far Reaching," *Alaska Economic Trends* (Alaska Dept. of Labor, Juneau), Jan. 1997.
8. Unemployment and population from Alaska Dept. of Labor, *www.labor.state.ak.us/research/emp_ue/ktlf.htm*, Feb. 18, 1999; population also from private communications with Ketchikan school administrators. Real estate from James Wiedle, research analyst, Alaska Housing Finance Corp., Anchorage, private communication, Dec. 9, 1998. Timber and seafood employment from Alaska Dept. of Labor, op. cit. note 1. Ketchikan growth sectors from "Ketchikan Recovery Is Mixed," *Juneau Empire,* Mar. 23, 1998, and James MacPherson, "Leaving Ketchikan," *Juneau Empire,* Apr. 6, 1998; tourism growth only, from Bob Newel, finance director, City of Ketchikan, private communication, Nov. 23, 1998.
9. Seasonal workers from ECO Northwest, op. cit. note 1.
10. Montana tourism from David Seideman, "Out of the Woods," *Audubon,* Jul./Aug. 1996. Northwest travel industry from B.C. Stats, "Special Focus: Tourism GDP, 1996," *Tourism Room Revenue,* Aug. 1997; Dean Runyan Associates, "Idaho Travel Impacts, 1997," "Oregon Travel Impacts, 1991–1997," and Washington

Travel Impacts, 1991–1998," all at *www.dra-research.com,* Feb. 25, 1999. Resource industry gross state or provincial product from B.C. Stats, "Industry Account, Goods Sector," *www.bcstats.gov.bc.ca/data/bus_stat/bcea/tab05.htm,* Feb. 19, 1999; U.S. Bureau of Economic Analysis, "State GSP by Industry," *www.bea.doc.gov/gsp/gspdata/,* Feb. 18, 1999. Trips for business and leisure (leisure includes family visits and tourism) estimated from U.S. Bureau of Transportation Statistics, *1995 American Travel Survey* (Washington, D.C.: Dept. of Transportation, 1997); Steve Kiehl, aviation planner, Puget Sound Regional Council, Seattle, private communication, Apr. 5, 1999; and McDowell Group, *Alaska Visitor Industry Economic Study* (Juneau: Tourism Division, Alaska Dept. of Commerce and Economic Development, 1998).

11. Local jobs from ECO Northwest, op. cit. note 1. Tourism's predictability from Jim Howe et al., *Balancing Nature and Commerce in Gateway Communities* (Washington, D.C.: Island Press, 1997). Wage scales from Thomas Michael Power, *Lost Landscapes and Failed Economies: The Search for a Value of Place* (Washington, D.C.: Island Press, 1996).
12. Passenger boat resource efficiency from Oak Ridge National Laboratory, *Transportation Energy Data Book* (Washington, D.C.: U.S. Dept. of Energy, 1998), and *www.cta-ornl.gov/publications/tedb.html,* and Michael Brower and Warren Leon, *The Consumer's Guide to Effective Environmental Choices* (New York: Three Rivers Press, 1999). Oil dumping from Douglas Frantz, "Cruise Line Pleads Guilty in Dumping," *New York Times,* Mar. 23, 1999. Tourism's share of driving estimated from Ralph Cipriani, planning manager, Puget Sound Regional Council, Seattle, private communication, Apr. 1, 1999; Bureau of Transportation Statistics, op. cit. note 10; and James MacKenzie, "Driving the Road to Sustainable Ground Transportation," in Roger Dower et al., *Frontiers of Sustainability: Environmentally Sound Agriculture, Forestry, Transportation, and Power Production* (Washington, D.C.: Island Press, 1997). Tourism's share of air travel estimated from Bureau of Transportation Statistics, op. cit. note 10; McDowell Group, op. cit. note 10; and Kiehl, op. cit. note 10. Tourism's share of greenhouse gas emissions estimated from spreadsheets assembled by NEW, as detailed in John C. Ryan, *Over Our Heads: A Local Look at Global Climate* (Seattle: NEW, 1997).

13. Private sector employment trends and relative industry employment from Alaska Dept. of Labor, op. cit. note 1; McDowell Group, op. cit. note 10; and ECO Northwest, op. cit. note 1.
14. Mills and mines from U.S. Bureau of the Census, *County Business Patterns* (Washington, D.C.: Dept. of Commerce, various years); Statistics Canada, *Canadian Forestry Statistics* (Ottawa: various years); and Jim Lewis, statistics manager, Resource Development Division, B.C. Ministry of Energy and Mines, Victoria, private communication, Feb. 8, 1999. Fishing boats from U.S. National Marine Fisheries Service, *Fisheries of the United States* (Silver Spring, Md.: Dept. of the Interior, various years); Oregon Dept. of Fish and Wildlife, *Pounds and Value of Commercially Caught Fish and Shellfish Landed in Oregon* (Portland: various years); and Dept. of Fisheries and Oceans, *Commercial License Status Report Pacific Region* (Ottawa: various years). Farms from U.S. National Agricultural Statistics Service (NASS), *www.usda.gov/nass,* U.S. Dept. of Agriculture, Washington, D.C., early 1999; NASS, "1996 Washington Annual Bulletin," *www.nass.usda.xgov/wa/farms96,* early 1999; NASS, "Idaho Agricultural Statistics Publications," *www.nass.usda.gov/id/nofarms97,* early 1999; Oregon Agriculture and Fisheries Statistics, "Number of Farms and Land in Farms: Oregon, 1960–1997," *www.oda.state.or.us/oass/bul0397.htm,* early 1999; and Statistics Canada, *Historical Overview of Canadian Agriculture 1997* (Ottawa: 1997). Mining employment—and employment data by industry throughout this book—from U.S. Bureau of Economic Analysis, *Regional Economic Informational System [REIS],1969–1996* (CD-ROM) (Washington, D.C.: Dept. of Commerce, 1998); REIS data posted at *fisher.lib.virginia.edu/spi* and *fisher.lib.virginia.edu/reis/county.html;* B.C. Stats, Victoria, *www.bcstats.gov.bc.ca;* and B.C. Stats, unpublished data based on Statistics Canada "Labour Force Survey," provided to NEW in Sept. 1998. In following notes, these data referred to as "NEW industry employment data."
15. Job trends by industry from 1979 to 1997 from NEW industry employment data, op. cit. note 14; updated for timber industry from Justine Hunter and Lori Culbert, "B.C. Forestry Loses 15,500 Jobs," *Vancouver Sun,* Jul. 16, 1998; and Peter Sleeth and Elisa Williams, "Laid-off Tech, Timber Workers Face Similar Fates," *Oregonian,* Sept. 6, 1998. Income trends by industry from Pat Bluernel, Data Services, B.C. Stats, Victoria, unpublished data,

late 1998; Bureau of Economic Analysis, op. cit. note 14; and REIS data posted at *fisher.lib.virginia.edu/cgi-local/reisbin/county2.cgi,* late 1998. In following notes, these data referred to as "NEW industry income data."

16. Job rankings from NEW industry employment data, op. cit. note 14. Personal income rankings from NEW industry income data, op. cit. note 15. Geographic distribution from Ray Rasker and Ben Alexander, *The New Challenge: People, Commerce and the Environment in the Yellowstone to Yukon Region* (Washington, D.C.: Wilderness Society, 1997); Ray Rasker, *A New Home on the Range: Economic Realities in the Columbia River Basin* (Washington, D.C.: Wilderness Society, 1995); and Gundars Rudzitis et al., "Snapshots of a Changing Northwest," Dept. of Geography, Univ. of Idaho, Moscow, 1997.
17. Unemployment rates from state and provincial employment agencies and press reports.
18. Labor force from Coldwell, op. cit. note 3; Hannum, op. cit. note 3; Wines, op. cit. note 3; and Lux, op. cit. note 3. Unpaid work from Melissa Benn, "Livelihood: Work in the New Urban Economy," Comedia and Demos, London, 1998.
19. Where northwesterners work from Rona Blumenthal, Office of Research, Evaluation, and Statistics, Social Security Administration, Washington, D.C., private communication, Jan. 22, 1998; Coldwell, op. cit. note 3; Hannum, op. cit. note 3; Wines, op. cit. note 3; Lux, op. cit. note 3; Paul Gosh, B.C. Stats, Ministry of Finance and Corporate Relations, Victoria, private communication, Jan. 22, 1999; and Ken LeVasseur, senior economist, Bureau of Labor Statistics, U.S. Dept. of Labor, Washington, D.C., private communication, Feb. 17, 1999.
20. Part-time workers from sources in note 19. Temporary workers from Washington Employment Security Dept., "Temporary Help Supply Employment in Washington," *www.wa.gov/esd/lmea/sprepts/newsp/temphelp.htm,* Feb. 22, 1999; and Governor's Tax Review Technical Advisory Committee, "Review of Oregon's Tax System," Office of the Governor, Salem, Jun. 1998. Self-employment from *B.C. Stats Infoline,* at *www.bcstats.gov.bc.ca,* Aug. 14, 1998.
21. Quality of life's economic role from Power, op. cit. note 11; Rasker and Alexander, op. cit. note 16; Rasker, op. cit. note 16; Gundars Rudzitis, *Wilderness and the Changing American West* (New York: Wiley, 1996); Gundars Rudzitis, "Towards a Theory of Place in

the 'New' American West," Dept. of Geography, Univ. of Idaho, Moscow, 1998; Christy Watrous Dearien and Gundars Rudzitis, "A Micro-Macro Model of Migration in the American Northwest," Dept. of Geography, Univ. of Idaho, Moscow, 1998; and Ernie Niemi and Ed Whitelaw (ECO Northwest, Eugene, Ore.), "Assessing Economic Tradeoffs in Forest Management," Pacific Northwest Research Station, U.S. Forest Service, Aug. 1997.

22. To compare the environmental impacts of different industries in the Northwest, we looked at aggregate impacts per dollar of economic output, measured in gross state or provincial product (from Bureau of Economic Analysis, op. cit. note 3, and B.C. Stats, "British Columbia Economic Accounts," op. cit. note 3). Energy consumption by industry nationally in Canada and the United States from U.S. Energy Information Administration, "1994 Manufacturing Energy Consumption Survey," *www.eia.doe.gov/emeu/consumption;* Robert Adler, Energy Information Administration, Washington, D.C., private communication, Mar. 23, 1999; and Canadian Industrial Energy End-Use Data and Analysis Centre, "Industrial Consumption of Energy Survey, 1990–1997," *www.cieedac.sfu.ca,* Simon Fraser University, Burnaby, B.C., Apr. 1, 1999. Water consumption from U.S. Geological Survey, *1995, USGS Open-File Report* 97-645 (Reston, Va.: 1997), also at *water.usgs.gov/public/watuse/;* and Chris Morgan, Water Management Branch, B.C. Ministry of Environment, Lands and Parks, Victoria, Apr. 17, 1999. Habitat disruption from John C. Ryan, *State of the Northwest* (Seattle: NEW, 1994), and Brower and Leon, op. cit. note 12. Toxics from U.S. Environmental Protection Agency, "TRI On- and Off-site Releases by Industry, 1996" and "State Fact Sheets," at *www.epa.gov/opptintr/tri/;* Environment Canada, "National Pollutant Release Inventory, 1996," at *www.ec.gc.ca/pdb/npri/;* Environment Canada, "NPRI 1996 British Columbia Fact Sheet," provided by Ed Wituschek, Environment Canada, Vancouver, B.C., Apr. 1999; Washington Dept. of Ecology, "Washington State Toxic Release Inventory Summary Report," provided by Idell Hansen, Dept. of Ecology, Olympia, Apr. 1999; and information from the Right to Know Network, *www.rtk.net.* Air emissions from U.S. Environmental Protection Agency, *National Emissions Trends Viewer CD, 1985–1995,* version 1 (Washington, D.C.: 1996). Water pollution from Dan Wrye, Alternative Strategies Unit, Wash. Dept. of Ecology, Olympia, private communications, Nov. 1997; Versna

Kontic, "Inventory of Authorized Discharges under the Waste Management Permit Fees Regulation," Univ. of Victoria, fall 1996; Oregon Dept. of Environmental Quality, "Oregon's 1998 Water Quality Status Assessment Report, Section 305(b) Report," Portland, 1998, also at *waterquality.deq.state.or.us/wq/305bRpt/305bReport.htm;* and Steve Butkus, "1998 Washington State Water Quality Assessment, Section 305(b) Report," Water Quality Program, Wash. Dept. of Ecology, Aug. 1997. Employment from NEW industry employment data, op. cit. note 14.

23. Sources cited in note 22.
24. Sources cited in note 22.
25. Shares of driving from MacKenzie, op. cit. note 12.
26. Investments from Nicholas D. Kristof, "Experts Question Roving Flow of Global Capital," *New York Times,* Sept. 20, 1998.
27. "Exportopia" from Ed Hunt, "Nations Worth Fighting For," *www.tidepool.org/hpnations.html.* Washington trade dependence from Bruce Ramsey, "Export-Dependent Washington Is Vulnerable to Recession," *Seattle Post-Intelligencer,* Oct. 7, 1998. B.C. Stats, "British Columbia Hardest Hit by Slumping Asian Exports," *B.C. Stats Infoline,* at *www.bcstats.gov.bc.ca,* May 22, 1998.
28. Washington cross-boundary expenditures from Robert A. Chase et al., *Washington State Input-Output 1987 Study* (Olympia: Office of Financial Management, 1993). Portland, Seattle, and Idaho Falls from David Holland and Bruce Weber, "Introduction," in Western Rural Development Center, "Rural-Urban Interdependence and Natural Resource Policy," Oregon State Univ., Corvallis, May 1996.
29. B.C. Big-box retailers from *B.C. Stats Infoline,* at *www.bcstats.gov.bc.ca,* Sept. 25, 1998. Rural business consolidation from Mark Drabenstott and Tim R. Smith, "The Changing Economy of the Rural Heartland," in Federal Reserve Bank of Kansas City, *Economic Forces Shaping the Rural Heartland* (Kansas City, Mo.: 1996).
30. Roles of shifting consumption and globalization from Hilary F. French, *Costly Tradeoffs: Reconciling Trade and the Environment* (Washington, D.C.: Worldwatch Institute, 1993); Robert Repetto, *Jobs, Competitiveness, and Environmental Regulation: What Are the Real Issues?* (Washington, D.C.: World Resources Institute, 1995); and E. B. Goodstein, *Jobs and the Environment: The Myth of a National Trade-off* (Washington, D.C.: Economic Policy Institute, 1994). Energy consumption per capita from U.S. Energy

Information Administration, *State Energy Data Report,* various editions (Washington, D.C.: Dept. of Energy, various years); and Statistics Canada, *Quarterly Report on Energy Supply-Demand in Canada,* various editions (Ottawa: various years). Per capita resource consumption trends from Eric D. Larson (Center for Energy and Environmental Studies, Princeton Univ., Princeton, N.J.), "Trends in the Consumption of Energy-Intensive Basic Materials in Industrialized Countries and Implications for Developing Regions," paper for International Symposium on Environmentally Sound Energy Technologies and Their Transfer to Developing Countries and European Economies in Transition, Milan, Italy, Oct. 21–25, 1991; and data provided by Grecia Matos, Minerals and Materials Analysis Section, U.S. Geological Survey, Reston, Va., Jul. 27, 1998.

31. Importance of connecting rural and urban areas from William A. Galston and Karen J. Baehler, *Rural Development in the United States* (Washington, D.C.: Island Press, 1995).
32. Urban population from NEW population data, op. cit. note 3; urbanizing trends from Galston and Baehler, op. cit. note 31.
33. Rural disadvantages from Galston and Baehler, op. cit. note 31, and Impresa, Inc., "Understanding the Two Oregons: Myths, Realities and Confronting Change," Portland Metropolitan Chamber of Commerce, Jan. 1999. Performance of greater Vancouver and province from H. Craig Davis and Thomas A. Hutton, "Structural Change in the British Columbia Economy: Regional Diversification and Metropolitan Transition," B.C. Round Table on the Environment and the Economy, Aug. 1992, and NEW population data, op. cit. note 3.
34. Rural strengths from Kenneth M. Johnson and Calvin L. Beale, "The Rural Rebound Revisited," *American Demographics,* Jul. 1995, and Calvin L. Beale, "Nonmetro Population Rebound: Still Real but Diminishing," *Rural Conditions and Trends,* vol. 9(2). Counties' fortunes from Rudzitis et al., op. cit. note 16.
35. Canadian Labour Congress, Dept. of Health, Safety and Environment, "Report by the Just Transition Working Group to the CLC Executive Council," third draft, Mar. 1999.
36. Log prices from Gina Binole, "Wood Products Outlook 'Dismal' on West Coast," *Portland Business Journal,* Nov. 2, 1998. Other commodity prices from Scott Sunde and Bill Virgin, "Price Drop Hits Growers Hard," *Seattle Post-Intelligencer,* Dec. 8, 1998. B.C.

layoffs from Gordon Hamilton, "Logging Closure Idles Another 1,000," *Vancouver Sun,* Nov. 6, 1998.

37. Downward ratchets of timber industry from Power, op. cit. note 11. Expectations of timber industry from Joel Connelly, "B.C. Facing Hard Truth," *Seattle Post-Intelligencer,* Jan. 12, 1999.
38. Government estimate of timber dependence from Garry Horne and Charlotte Powell, "Community Economic Dependencies," Analysis and Evaluation Branch, Treasury Board, Ministry of Finance and Corporate Relations, Victoria, Feb. 1995. Scholarly review from Andrew Krikelas, "Why Regions Grow: A Review of Research on the Economic Base Model," *Economic Review* (Federal Reserve Bank of Atlanta), Jul./Aug. 1992.
39. Recent misuse of economic base model includes a widely reported study commissioned by the Oregon Business Council claiming the timber industry constitutes "one-fourth of Oregon's economic base" (Gina Binole, "Study Underscores Value of State's Forestry Industry," *Portland Business Journal,* Feb. 23, 1998); a U.S. government report on the Columbia River basin claiming, "It is the basic or export industries that add to the level of income and employment in a community" (Interior Columbia Basin Ecosystem Management Project, *Economic and Social Conditions of Communities* [Boise: U.S. Forest Service and U.S. Bureau of Land Management, 1998]); and the B.C. government's reports claiming that the "true" economic role of resource industries equals twice the industries' jobs, while the true role of the service industries is about half those industries' job count (Ministry of Finance and Corporate Relations, Planning and Statistics Division, "The Structure of the British Columbia Economy: A Land-Use Perspective," B.C. Round Table, Mar. 1991, and Horne and Powell, op. cit. note 38).
40. Comparison with global growth rate from Alan Thein Durning and Christopher D. Crowther, *Misplaced Blame: The Real Roots of Population Growth* (Seattle: NEW, 1997). County population change from NEW population data, op. cit. note 3.
41. Usage of *urban* and *rural* here corresponds to *metropolitan* and *nonmetropolitan* in census terminology. Population change from NEW population data, op. cit. note 3.
42. Employers' quality-of-life preferences from Jerry D. Johnson and Ray Rasker, "The Role of Economic and Quality of Life Values in Rural Business Location," *Journal of Rural Studies,* 1995, and William Beyers and David Lindahl, "Lone Eagles and High Fliers

in Rural Producer Services," *Rural Development Perspectives,* vol. 11(3), 1996. Population-jobs relationship from Power, op. cit. note 11; Stephen M. Meyer, *Environmentalism and Economic Prosperity: Testing the Environmental Impact Hypothesis* (Cambridge, Mass.: MIT Press, 1992); Rudzitis, *Wilderness and the Changing American West,* op. cit. note 21; and Dearien and Rudzitis, op. cit. note 21. Protected wildlands and local economy from Rudzitis et al., op. cit. note 16.

43. Timber families' work from Annabel Kirschner Cook, "Increasing Poverty in Timber-Dependent Areas in Western Washington," *Society and Natural Resources*, vol. 8, pp. 97–109, 1995.
44. Commitment to place from Rudzitis, op. cit. note 21. Entrepreneurial local leaders from Ernie Niemi and Ed Whitelaw (ECO Northwest, Eugene, Ore.), "The Potential Social and Economic Impacts of Long-Rotation Timber Management," paper at High Quality Forestry Workshops: The Idea of Long Rotations, 1994.
45. Whitefish income from Power, op. cit. note 11.
46. Pensions from Galston and Baehler, op. cit. note 31. Other qualities of retirement economies from Power, op. cit. note 11.
47. Women in influential positions from B.C. Stats, "Focus on BC's Labour Market: Integration of the Sexes," *B.C. Stats Infoline,* at *www.bcstats.gov.bc.ca,* Jul. 1998.
48. Growth of elder population from *B.C. Stats Infoline,* at *www.bcstats.gov.bc.ca,* Feb. 27, 1998. New retiree settlement pattern from William Riebsame, ed., *Atlas of the New West: Portrait of a Changing Region* (New York: Norton, 1997).
49. Rare species in Haida Gwaii from Richard Cannings and Sydney Cannings, *British Columbia: A Natural History* (Vancouver: Greystone, 1996).
50. Michael M'Gonigle and Ben Parfitt, *Forestopia: A Practical Guide to the New Forest Economy* (Madeira Park, B.C.: Harbour, 1994).
51. B.C. Wild, "Taking It All Away," Vancouver, B.C., Mar. 1996.
52. Economic plight of timber towns from Power, op. cit. note 11; Cook, op. cit. note 43; and Christine Overdevest and Gary Green, "Forest Dependence and Community Well-Being: A Segmented Market Approach," *Society and Natural Resources*, vol. 8, pp. 111–131, 1995.
53. Islands Community Stability Initiative (ICSI), "Consensus Documents," *www.spruceroots.org/ICSI,* late 1998.

54. Local control from Jonathan Kusel and Louise Fortmann, "Well-Being in Forest-Dependent Communities" (2 vols.), Dept. of Forestry and Resource Management, Univ. of California, Berkeley, Sept. 1991.
55. Haida Gwaii jobs per log from B.C. Wild, op. cit. note 51. Limits of value-added manufacturing from Galston and Baehler, op. cit. note 31. Urban resource jobs from Niemi and Whitelaw, op. cit. note 21, and Davis and Hutton, op. cit. note 33.
56. Jobs per board foot from Select Standing Committee on Forests, Energy, Mines and Petroleum Resources, "Lumber Remanufacturing in British Columbia," Parliament, Victoria, 1993. Furniture employment from Catherine Mater, vice-president, Mater Engineering, Ltd., presentation at First North American Conference on Trade in Sustainable Forest Products, Washington, D.C., May 26, 1993.
57. Total employment in value-added manufacturing from Dave Katz, "Modeling a Small-Scale Secondary Manufacturing Timber Industry for Southeast Alaska," Southeast Alaska Conservation Council, Juneau, Aug. 1997; Bureau of the Census, op. cit. note 14; Rose Braden, research analyst, Center for International Trade in Forest Products, College of Forest Resources, University of Washington, Seattle, private communication, Apr. 23, 1999; and Mark Shepherd, provincial investment manager, Lower Mainland/Interior, Forest Renewal B.C., Vancouver, private communication, Apr. 23, 1999. Value-added trends in B.C. from B.C. Stats, "British Columbia Falling Behind in Export Boom for Secondary Manufactured Wood," *B.C. Stats Infoline,* at *www.bcstats.gov.bc.ca,* Jun. 12, 1998.
58. Logger dropout share from Power, op. cit. note 11.
59. Forest roads from John C. Ryan, "Roads Take Toll on Salmon, Grizzlies, Taxpayers," *NEW Indicator* (NEW, Seattle), Dec. 11, 1995. Other ecological degradation from Ryan, op. cit. note 22.
60. Brian Egan, "Ecological Restoration for British Columbia," *B.C. Environmental Report* (B.C. Environmental Network), fall 1998.
61. David Rains Wallace, *The Klamath Knot* (San Francisco: Sierra Club Books, 1984).
62. Cecilia Danks and Lynn Jungwirth, "Community-Based Socioeconomic Assessment and Monitoring of Activities Related to National Forest Management," Watershed Research and Training Center, Hayfork, Calif., Jul. 1998.

63. Timber industry's labor and payroll per unit of wood from Niemi and Whitelaw, op. cit. note 21.
64. Layoffs from Cecilia Danks and Sally Aldinger, "Trinity County Ecosystem Management Technician Training Program Summary and Review," Watershed Research and Training Center, Hayfork, Calif., Oct. 1998.
65. Billionaires from "The World's Richest People," *Forbes,* Jul. 6, 1998. Number of millionaires and distribution of wealth in Northwest estimated from Armine Yalnizyan, *The Growing Gap: A Report on Growing Inequality between the Rich and Poor in Canada* (Toronto: Centre for Social Justice, 1998); Statistics Canada, Publication Catalogue 13-207-XPB; and Lawrence Mishel et al., *State of Working America 1998–99* (Ithaca, N.Y.: Cornell Univ. Press, 1999). Early 1999 billionaires' net worth estimated from press reports and prevailing stock prices.
66. Specialists track income disparities among families with children to allow comparisons undistorted by changing age structure of the population. Average incomes by class, in constant 1996 dollars, from Kathryn Larin and Elizabeth McNichol, "Pulling Apart: A State-by-State Analysis of Income Trends," Center on Budget and Policy Priorities, Washington, D.C., Dec. 16, 1997. Not counted are capital gains and fringe benefits, which accrue overwhelmingly to high-income families; see Peter Passell, "Benefits Dwindle Along with Wages for the Unskilled," *New York Times,* Jun. 14, 1998.
67. Wage figures, in 1997 dollars, and CEO earnings from Mishel et al., op. cit. note 65.
68. Canadian income distribution trends from Yalnizyan, op. cit. note 65; *B.C. Stats Infoline,* at *www.bcstats.gov.bc.ca,* Oct. 2, 1998. Women's work from B.C. Stats, "BC's Labour Market—the New Reality," *B.C. Stats Infoline,* at *www.bcstats.gov.bc.ca,* Jan. 23, 1998, and Chinhui Juhn and Kevin M. Murphy, "Inequality in Labor Market Outcomes: Contrasting the 1980s and Earlier Decades," *Economic Policy Review* (Federal Reserve Bank of New York), Jan. 1995.
69. B.C.'s dampening of inequalities from Fiona MacPhail, "Increased Economic Inequality in Canada: Is B.C. Any Different?" *B.C. Commentary* (Canadian Centre for Policy Alternatives, Vancouver), summer 1998. Widening Canadian disparities from Yalnizyan, op. cit. note 65. Eighties-nineties comparison in North-

west states from Larin and McNichol, op. cit. note 66. Recent improvements from Lawrence Mishel et al., "Finally, Real Wage Gains," Economic Policy Institute, Jul. 17, 1998. Washington's recent narrowing of income gaps from James L. McIntire, "Family Income Disparities in Washington State," Fiscal Policy Center, Graduate School of Public Affairs, Univ. of Washington, Jan. 1998.

70. Troubles with locally funded training from Galston and Baehler, op. cit. note 31. Mobility-education relationship from Larry Long, *Migration and Residential Mobility in the United States* (New York: Russell Sage Foundation, 1988).
71. Danks and Jungwirth, op. cit. note 62.
72. Nontimber forest products industry from David Foster, "Money Doesn't Grow on Trees," *Bellingham Herald,* Mar. 3, 1998.
73. Educational attainment of B.C. workers from B.C. Stats, "BC's Labour Market," op. cit. note 68. Dropouts from Alan Eck, "Job-Related Education and Training: Their Impact on Earnings," *Monthly Labor Review,* Oct. 1993.
74. Occupational shifts from Ronald E. Kutscher, "Historical Trends, 1950–92, and Current Uncertainties," *Monthly Labor Review,* Nov. 1993, and B.C. Stats, "BC's Labour Market," op. cit. note 68.
75. Bifurcation from Kutscher, op. cit. note 74, and Eck, op. cit. note 73.
76. Inequality and technology from John Bound and George Johnson, "What Are the Causes of Rising Wage Inequality in the United States?" *Economic Policy Review* (Federal Reserve Bank of New York), Jan. 1995, and Juhn and Murphy, op. cit. note 68.
77. Inequality and immigration from James P. Smith and Barry Edmonston, eds., *The New Americans* (Washington, D.C.: National Academy of Sciences, 1997), and George J. Borjas, "The New Economics of Immigration," *Atlantic Monthly*, Nov. 1996.
78. Inequality and trade from Gary Burtless, "International Trade and the Rise in Earnings Inequality," *Journal of Economic Literature,* Jun. 1995.
79. Union membership for Northwest states estimated from U.S. Bureau of the Census, *Statistical Abstract of the United States: 1995* (Washington, D.C.: 1995). B.C. estimated from Canadian Centre for Policy Alternatives, "What's Happening to Incomes?" *B.C. Commentary,* summer 1998.
80. Share of Northwest workers earning poverty wage estimated from Mishel et al., op. cit. note 65, as weighted average of Idaho, Ore., and Wash. on basis of state populations from NEW population

data, op. cit. note 3. Minimum wage and inequality from Fiona MacPhail, "What Caused Earnings Inequality to Increase in Canada During the 1980s?" *Cambridge Journal of Economics*, forthcoming. Poverty budget from John E. Schwarz, "The Hidden Side of the Clinton Economy," *Atlantic Monthly*, Oct. 1998.

81. Importance of assets from Bruce Ackerman and Anne Alstott, *The Stakeholder Society* (New Haven, Conn.: Yale Univ. Press, 1999).
82. Nonlabor share of income from NEW industry income data, op. cit. note 15. Higher profits from Mishel et al., op. cit. note 65.
83. Alan Thein Durning and Yoram Bauman, *Tax Shift* (Seattle: NEW, 1998).
84. Government jobs from NEW industry employment data, op. cit. note 14; government personal income from NEW industry income data, op. cit. note 15.
85. Carbon storage from Jerry Franklin, "Pacific Northwest Forests," in Michael Barbour and William Billings, eds., *North American Terrestrial Vegetation* (Cambridge, U.K.: Cambridge Univ. Press, 1988).
86. Northwest's environmental industries estimated from Environmental Business International, "Environmental Industry Overview," San Diego, Calif., 1996; Thomas A. Hutton, "Economic Implications of Environmental Enhancement: A Review and Interpretation of the Contemporary Literature," Center for Human Settlements, School of Community and Regional Planning, Univ. of British Columbia, Sept. 1995; and Dept. of Community, Trade and Economic Development (CTED), *The Next Generation of Energy: The Renewable Energy and Energy Efficiency Industries in Washington State* (Olympia: 1998). Rates of growth in environmental industries from David R. Berg and Grant Ferrier, *Meeting the Challenge: U.S. Industry Faces the 21st Century: The U.S. Environmental Industry* (Washington, D.C.: U.S. Office of Technology Policy, 1998), and Benjamin Goldman, *Sustainable America: New Public Policy for the 21st Century* (Washington, D.C.: U.S. Economic Development Administration, 1995).
87. CTED, op. cit. note 86.
88. Site described in John Schaeffer et al., *A Place in the Sun* (White River Junction, Vt.: Chelsea Green, 1997).
89. Ballard employees from Debby Roman, public relations manager, Ballard Power Systems, Burnaby, B.C., private communication, Mar. 28, 1999.

90. Real Goods online catalog at *www.realgoods.com.*
91. Todd Litman and Felix Laube, "Automobile Dependency and Economic Development," paper presented at Transportation Research Board 1999 Annual Meeting, available from Victoria Transport Policy Institute, *www.islandnet.com/~litman.*
92. Transit and gasoline spending impacts from Litman and Laube, op. cit. note 91.
93. Northwest expenditures on motor vehicles from State of Idaho, *www2.state.id.us/itd/econ/econpage.htm,* Jan. 4 and Apr. 8, 1999; DesRosiers Auto Research, Ontario, private communication, Feb. 22, 1999; and Dick Hauser, economic analyst, Washington Dept. of Licensing, Olympia, private communications, Dec. 18, 1998, and Mar. 3, 1999. Oregon estimated from Polk Company, "Auto Tracker Statistical Report," Southfield, Mich., various editions. Price per vehicle derived from Washington data. Petroleum and natural gas expenditures from National Energy Information Center, "Energy Price and Expenditure Estimates by Source, 1970–1995," *www.eia.doe.gov,* Apr. 19, 1999; Energy Information Administration, op. cit. note 30; and Colette Craig, National Energy Board, Calgary, Alberta, private communication, Feb. 15, 1999. Sales of timber, farm products, fish, and minerals based on industry gross state or provincial products from B.C. Stats, "British Columbia Economic Accounts," op. cit. note 3, and Bureau of Economic Analysis, op. cit. note 10. A more sophisticated measure of the region's balance of trade in resource-heavy goods would reflect the share of regional car, oil, and gas expenditures that remains in the regional economy and the share of locally produced resource commodities sold to local buyers. Northwest's out-of-region expenditures on fossil fuels and vehicles ($19 billion) exceeding out-of-region sales of resource commodities ($12 billion to $18 billion) estimated using import and export ratios for each industry from Chase et al., op. cit. note 28.
94. Farm income from Oregon Employment Dept., *1998 Regional Economic Profile, Region 10* (Salem: 1997).
95. Farm income from 1987 Census of Agriculture in Power, op. cit. note 11.
96. Visitors to parks estimated from U.S. National Parks Service, *1996 Statistical Abstract* (Washington, D.C.: Dept. of the Interior, 1997). Visitors to wilderness from David N. Cole, *Wilderness Recreation Use Trends, 1966 through 1994* (Ogden, Utah: U.S. Forest Service,

Intermountain Research Station, 1996). Joke about recreationist from Howe et al., op. cit. note 11. Recreation industry in interior Columbia River basin, portion east of Cascade crest and south of Canadian border, from Pacific Northwest Research Station, *Status of the Interior Columbia Basin, Summary of Scientific Findings* (Portland, Ore.: U.S. Forest Service, 1996). Spending on wildlife-related recreation from U.S. Fish and Wildlife Service and U.S. Bureau of the Census, *1996 National Survey of Fishing, Hunting, and Wildlife-Associated Recreation* (Washington, D.C.: Depts. of the Interior and Commerce, 1998). Mining gross state product from Bureau of Economic Analysis, op. cit. note 10.

97. Kevin Heubusch, "Small Is Beautiful," *American Demographics,* Jan. 1998.
98. Compact neighborhoods' effects on driving from Alan Thein Durning, *The Car and the City* (Seattle: NEW, 1996).
99. Timothy H. Hill (Central Oregon Community College, Bend), "Select Visitor-Related Impacts in Deschutes County," City of Bend and Bend Chamber of Commerce, Jan. 15, 1993.
100. Priscilla Salant et al., "Lone Eagles among Washington's In-Migrants: Who Are They and Are They Moving to Rural Places?" *Northwest Journal of Business and Economics,* 1997, pp. 1–16.
101. Oregon Employment Dept., op. cit. note 94.
102. High-tech employment conservatively estimated from B.C. Stats, "British Columbia High Technology Sector, 1988–1996," Victoria, 1997; William B. Beyers and Peter B. Nelson (Dept. of Geography, Univ. of Washington, Seattle), *The Economic Impact of Technology-Based Industries in Washington State in 1997* (Seattle: Technology Alliance, 1998); and American Electronics Association, Oregon Council et al., *1998 Oregon Technology Benchmarks* (Portland, Ore.: 1998). Data for each state or province based on different definitions of high tech. Washington study most authoritative, defining high tech as does the National Science Foundation—those industries in which more than 10 percent of workers are in research and development—while B.C. and Oregon focus estimates on computer and electronics industries. Applying this definition to entire Northwest would yield higher jobs estimate.
103. Washington high-tech sector from Beyers and Nelson, op. cit. note 102. Average software earnings include value of stock options.
104. Oregon high-tech growth from American Electronics Association, Oregon Council et al., op. cit. note 102. B.C. high tech from *B.C. Stats Infoline,* at *www.bcstats.gov.bc.ca,* Jun. 12, 1998.

105. Spending on computers from Goldman, op. cit. note 86. Washington households' computer ownership from Robert Baker, "The New State Population Survey," *LMI Review* (Washington State Employment Security Dept., Olympia), Feb. 1999.
106. Computer manufacturing's impacts from John C. Ryan and Alan Thein Durning, *Stuff: The Secret Lives of Everyday Things* (Seattle: NEW, 1997). Boeing aircraft's worldwide CO_2 emissions estimated from Boeing's global market share in passenger jets (more than 50 percent) and Mark Barrett, "Aircraft Pollution: Environmental Impacts and Future Solutions," World Wide Fund for Nature, Gland, Switzerland, Aug. 1991.
107. High-tech growth from Oregon Employment Dept., op. cit. note 94. Traits of companies from Oregon Innovation Center, "Gazelles in the High Desert: A Study of the Vitality and Needs of Central Oregon's Growing Technology Businesses," Redmond, Ore., Oct. 1998.
108. Retail consolidation from Drabenstott and Smith, op. cit. note 29.
109. Northwest auto deaths from Greg Hastings, Ore. State Police Dept., Portland, private communication, Jan. 5, 1998; Julie Macdonald, B.C. Vital Statistics Agency, Victoria, private communication, Dec. 23, 1997; Pat Starzik, Wash. Center for Health Statistics, Olympia, private communication, Jan. 27, 1998; Center for Health Statistics, *Washington State Vital Statistics 1996* (Olympia: Dept. of Health, 1997); and Idaho Center for Vital Statistics and Health Policy, *1996 Annual Summary of Vital Statistics* (Boise: 1997).
110. Deschutes County income from Oregon Employment Dept., op. cit. note 94. Northwest nonlabor income from NEW industry income data, op. cit. note 15.
111. Landscaping and ranching jobs from NEW industry employment data, op. cit. note 14.
112. Trailer dwellers from U.S. Bureau of the Census, "Aggregate Persons by Tenure by Units in Structure," *1990 Census, Summary Tape File 1A* (Washington, D.C.: Dept. of Commerce, 1992). Housing affordability from *B.C. Stats Infoline,* at *www.bcstats.gov.bc.ca,* Jul. 31, 1998.
113. Real estate trends from Riebsame, op. cit. note 48, and Seideman, op. cit. note 10.
114. Vacation homes and share of all houses from the *U.S. Census of Housing* for 1970, 1980, and 1990, data provided by Myra Washington, Physical and Social Characteristics Branch, Housing and

Household Economic Statistics Division, Bureau of the Census, U.S. Dept. of Commerce, Washington, D.C., Feb. 24, 1999.

115. Inheritance from Robert B. Avery and Michael S. Rendall, "Estimating the Size and Distribution of the Baby Boomers' Prospective Inheritances," Cornell Univ. Dept. of Consumer Economics and Housing, Ithaca, N.Y., 1993. Second-home market projections from Howe et al., op. cit. note 11.
116. Number of new residences estimated from U.S. Bureau of the Census, *Statistical Abstract of the United States 1998* (Washington, D.C.: Dept. of Commerce, 1998). Weight of house and share of resources from Steve Loken and Walter Spurling, *ReCraft 90: Construction of a Resource Efficient House* (Missoula, Mont.: Center for Resourceful Building Technology, 1993), and David Malin Roodman and Nicholas Lenssen, *A Building Revolution: How Ecology and Health Concerns Are Transforming Construction* (Washington, D.C.: Worldwatch Institute, 1995). Developed land area from U.S. Dept. of Agriculture, Natural Resource Conservation Service (NRCS), published and unpublished data from the National Resources Inventories of 1992, 1987, and 1982 provided to NEW by each state's NRCS office. Relative impacts on wildlife of housing and other land uses from Brower and Leon, op. cit. note 12. Land areas from Ryan, op. cit. note 22.
117. Capital gains in Oregon from Bruce Ramsey, "Export-Dependent Washington Is Vulnerable to Recession," *Seattle Post-Intelligencer,* Oct. 7, 1998. Top households' stock share from Mishel et al., op. cit. note 65. Share of households with stocks from Mishel et al., op. cit. note 65, and Yalnizyan, op. cit. note 65. Investment income of top 5 percent of households from Larin and McNichol, op. cit. note 66. B.C. investment income from *B.C. Stats Infoline,* at *www.bcstats.gov.bc.ca,* Aug. 21, 1998.
118. Juliet Schor, *The Overworked American* (New York: Basic, 1992).
119. Consumption impacts from Ryan and Durning, op. cit. note 106.
120. Snowmobile price from U.S. Fish and Wildlife Service, *1996 National and State Economic Impacts of Wildlife Watching* (Washington, D.C.: Dept. of the Interior, 1997). Personal watercraft price from Karla Hult, "Personal Watercraft Use Grows," *Juneau Empire,* Jun. 22, 1998. Numbers of personal watercraft and snowmobiles estimated on basis of national figures from George Hunter, "Resort Waits for Jet Ski Ban," *Eugene (Oregon) Register-Guard,* Jul. 20, 1998. Air and water pollution from Earth Island Insti-

tute, Bluewater Network, *www.earthisland.org/bw/,* summer 1998, and Brower and Leon, op. cit. note 12.

121. Sales and registrations of SUVs and other vehicles from Polk Company, op. cit. note 93. Off-road use of SUVs from Paul Rogers, "U.S. Fuel Efficiency Dropping," *San Jose Mercury News*, May 1, 1997, and Matt Sabo, "Why Do We Love Our SUVs?" *Bend (Oregon) Bulletin,* Mar. 21, 1999. Gas mileage from U.S. Environmental Protection Agency, *www.epa.gov/reg3artd/vehic/annem95.htm,* Washington, D.C., Aug. 11, 1998. Light trucks' effects on regional energy consumption estimated from U.S. Federal Highway Administration, *Highway Statistics, 1985* and *1997* (Washington, D.C.: Dept. of Transportation, 1986 and 1999), and Energy Information Administration, op. cit. note 30.

122. Registered RVs from private communications with Washington State Dept. of Motor Vehicles, Oregon Driver and Motor Vehicle Services, Idaho Transportation Dept., and B.C. Public Information Dept., summer 1998. Vehicle length from private communications with RV dealers. RV sales growth from *RV Business,* Dec. 1997. Baby-boom projections from Tom Seery, "Building a Baby-Boom Demand: Motor-Homes," *Seattle Times,* May 27, 1997.

123. Daily resource consumption from Ryan and Durning, op. cit. note 106. Planets' worth of resources from Mathis Wackernagel and William Rees, *Our Ecological Footprint: Reducing Human Impact on the Earth* (Gabriola Island, B.C.: New Society, 1996).

124. Energy consumption from Energy Information Administration, op. cit. note 30, and Statistics Canada, op. cit. note 30. Greenhouse gas emissions from Ryan, op. cit. note 12. Water consumption from Howard Perlman, hydrologist, U.S. Geological Survey, Reston, Va., private communication, Apr. 21, 1999, and Gary W. Robinson, Water Allocation Section, Water Management Branch, B.C. Ministry of Environment, Lands and Parks, Victoria, private communication, Jan. 4, 1999. Air and water pollution and toxic wastes from U.S. Environmental Protection Agency, "Our Northwest Environment 1997," Seattle, 1998, and B.C. Ministry of Environment, Lands and Parks and Environment Canada, *State of the Environment Report for British Columbia* (Victoria: 1993). Solid waste from Recycling Council of British Columbia and B.C. Ministry of Environment, Lands and Parks, Pollution Prevention and Remediation Branch, "B.C. Municipal Solid Waste Tracking Report 1996," Victoria, 1997; Washington Dept. of Ecology,

"Solid Waste in Washington State: Seventh Annual Status Report," *www.wa.gov/ecology/swfa/swfacts,* Olympia, Feb. 1999; and Oregon Dept. of Environmental Quality, "1997 Oregon Material Recovery Survey Report," *www.deq.state.or.us/wmc/solwaste/mrs97.html,* Portland, Mar. 20, 1999. National consumption trends from Larson, op. cit. note 30, and Matos, op. cit. note 30.

125. Potential of high tech from Ernst Von Weizsäcker et al., *Factor Four: Doubling Wealth, Halving Resource Use* (London: Earthscan, 1997).
126. Adelaide de Menil and William Reid, *Out of the Silence* (Fort Worth, Tex.: Amon Carter Museum of Western Art, 1971).
127. Motives for work from R. E. Lane, "Does Money Buy Happiness?" *Public Interest,* fall 1993, and Michael Argyle, *The Psychology of Happiness* (New York: Methuen, 1987).
128. Prison jobs from Durning and Crowther, op. cit. note 40.